D1710271

DOLLS TO MAKE
For Fun and Profit

THE AUTHOR WITH DOLLS YOU CAN MAKE

DOLLS TO MAKE
for Fun and Profit

By EDITH FLACK ACKLEY

Author of
"Marionettes: Easy to Make! Fun to Use!"

Drawings by
TELKA ACKLEY

J. B. LIPPINCOTT COMPANY

PHILADELPHIA   NEW YORK

To
S. W.

CONTENTS

A Letter to Whoever Opens this Book

This book is to help you to have some of the fun that I have had in making dolls.

I remember that when I was a child, we had a "rag doll" in our family. I don't dare say that it was mine first; it may have been made for my sister, Avis, but I played with it. Several people had a hand in the making (I know my father painted the face), so the doll had several names, Dumpling Corwin Case Flack, and she was the most lovable doll that ever lived!

One of the best Christmases I ever had was my little daughter's eighth. I spent about twenty evenings getting ready. I made clothes for every doll she owned, big and little, and for the bear, too.

There was a special little tree for the dolls that year, and each present was carefully wrapped and labeled. My daughter says she never had a happier Christmas. (But who really had the most fun? I'll bet I did!)

The first complete doll that I made was similar to these in the book, but stuffed with rags. I made it for my daughter, who was about a year old. It wasn't so very good, but it was my beginning. Since then I have made well over a thousand dolls, including those that were strung up for marionettes, and I'm not tired of them yet. I love making them!

I even had a doll shop one summer, the stock made up of just my own dolls.

Almost every morning I was up by five-thirty, getting a head start on the sewing.

I had two work tables, one by my dining-room window and one in the shop. I *worked!*

At the end of the summer before Labor Day, I had to close for lack of dolls, but I closed with an order for thirty-four dolls, ranging in price from two dollars to five.

I have made dolls for the stage. I have made caricatures of people, special dolls for special children, dolls for collectors, dolls for window displays and for advertising. They have been big ones and little ones, but all made like those in this book, that is, cloth stuffed with cotton, and faces made with darning cotton and thread.

All this talking about myself is just to give you an idea of what can be done with dolls for fun or money (or both!). Whether you wish to make just one doll for some little child, or wish to start a business for yourself, I hope that this simple book will help you.

EDITH FLACK ACKLEY.

THE BABY DOLL

The Pattern

TO MAKE your pattern use a piece of tracing paper or strong white tissue paper. Have it long enough to cover the full length of the baby—14 inches.

Place the paper over the upper half of the pattern and trace it with a pencil, then with lines A and B coin-

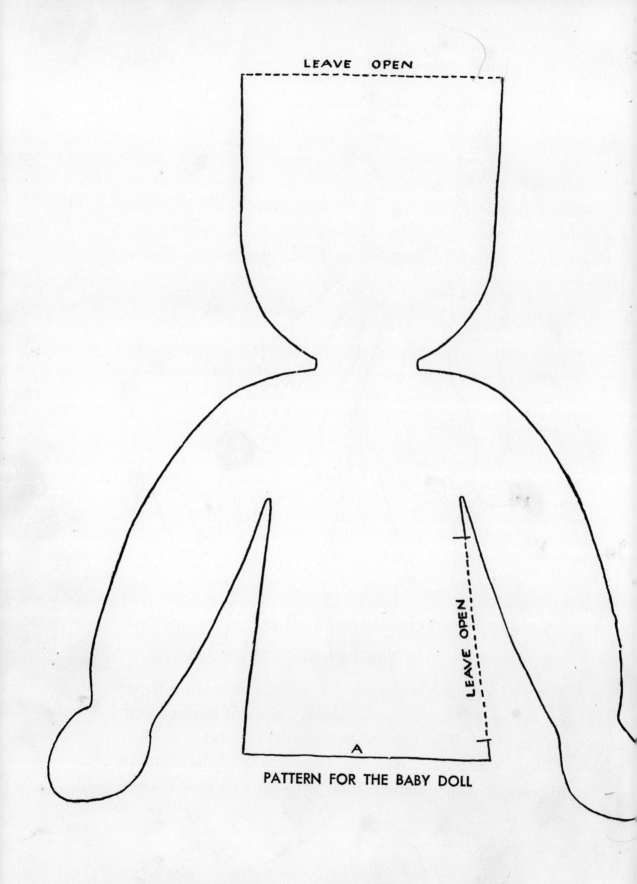

LEAVE OPEN

LEAVE OPEN

A

PATTERN FOR THE BABY DOLL

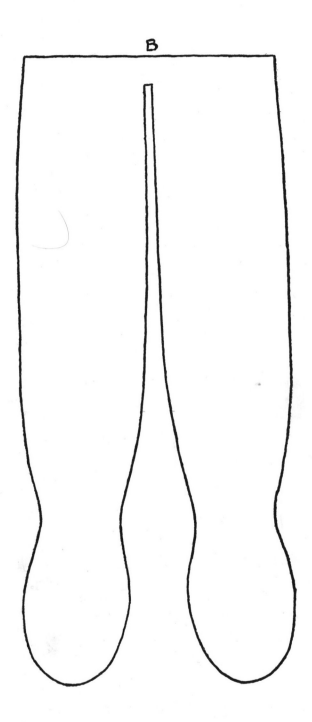

B

·3·

ciding, trace the lower half. Now cut it out on the pencil line.

If you would like to have a more substantial pattern, take a piece of drawing paper or ordinary brown wrapping paper. Place your thin pattern on it, draw around it, and then cut out the second pattern.

The material I like best for the body is any cotton or muslin material that stretches a little when you put the cotton in. The patterns for the clothes are made for a crepe doll, but there is not much difference in the size if you use muslin for the body.

Pin your pattern to a piece of "stretchable" material that has been folded lengthwise.

Draw around the pattern with a freshly sharpened pencil, having the line as light as possible. Do not cut it out till after you have sewed it.

Sewing and Stuffing

You can do the sewing on the machine if you are good at it (I am not) or sew it by hand. Whichever you do, sew just inside the line so that the needle won't drag the thread through the black mark and make the seam look dark.

Don't forget to leave one side seam and the top of the head open or you will have to sigh and rip.

Now cut the doll out, leaving a small seam, about an eighth of an inch. Overcast at the sides of the neck, the underarms and the crotch of the legs to keep the seams from raveling.

Now turn the body right side out, pulling the arms and legs through the side opening.

For stuffing the doll, use ordinary hospital cotton, which is called absorbent cotton. It is a smooth white cotton and it packs well. It it inexpensive, too.

It is easier on the neck seams if you stuff the cotton into legs, arms and body through the side opening. Use small pieces at a time and pack firmly.

Stuff the legs first. When you reach the top of the legs,

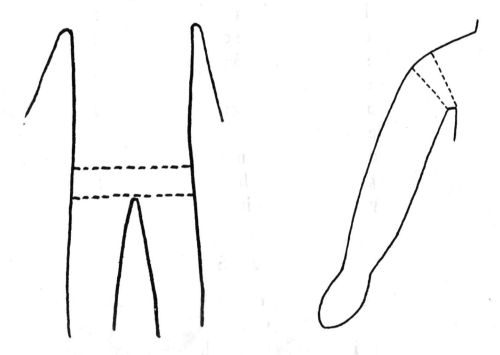

sew across the body, leave a space of about half an inch unstuffed, then sew across again. This is so the baby can sit down.

Force the feet forward (to look like real ones) and sew them up into position. If you are in doubt about the length, look at the pattern for the sole of the moccasin as a guide.

If you would like the arms flexible at the shoulders, sew across as illustrated.

Next, find a long wire nail or a stick to use in the neck. A regular kitchen match will do (light it and blow it out) but something a little longer and stronger is better.

Wrap it firmly with cotton until it is about the size of the neck. Wind the top end with thread, and insert it through the side opening. There is a sketch on page 28 to show how to do it. The stick should reach halfway up the head. As you have probably guessed, this is to keep the head from getting floppy after a week or so.

Next stuff the rest of the body and shoulders, coaxing them into a good smooth shape. Pack it quite solid, then sew up the side seam.

Spend a little time and use care with the head. If you insert a smooth thick sheet of the cotton between the face and the wrapped stick and pack in back of it, you will find it makes a better job than stuffing it in any old way.

Fold over the cloth at the top of the head, keeping in mind that a head looks round on the top, not square or thin and flat, and sew it so no corners will poke up through the hair.

The Hair

For the hair, use a very fine wool; if it has a luster, so much the better. Pale yellow, of course, seems most like a baby.

I wind off some of the wool on a magazine—going around about twelve times. I cut it across one end, which gives me a long strand of "hair" made up of about twelve

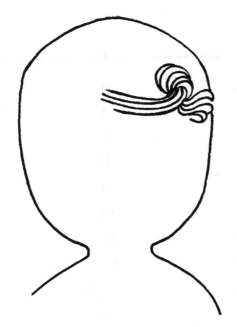

HOW TO SEW ON "HAIR" OF WOOL

THIS IDEA, BUT HAVE MORE STRANDS
AND THE LOOPS CLOSER TOGETHER

lengths of wool. When this is used up, I wind off more from my ball in the same way.

Use ordinary fine thread for sewing the curls to the head.

Start anywhere you like. I always start at the left side of a doll's head and frame the face, and then fill in the back. Very often I have to add a few ringlets in front after the features are on.

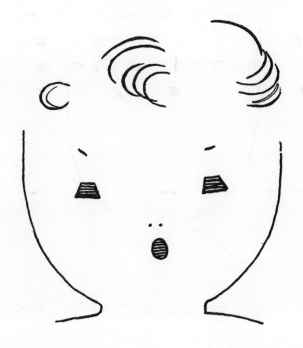

The Face

Trace the features onto tissue paper and lay it on the doll's face. You can poke your pencil point through the tissue and make small dots to show you where to put the eyes and mouth. You can guess at the nose and eyebrows.

Don't risk pencil smudges showing through the stitches. You aren't obliged to use the features in the drawing, of course. Experiment with other types of eyes, nose and mouth, if you like, but do it on tissue paper first.

For the eyes, I like a blue floss, the kind that comes in a small skein. I use two strands in my needle. Brown sewing cotton is good for the eyebrows and red sewing cotton for the mouth and nose. A red pencil gives the color to the cheeks. Try it on a piece of crepe first.

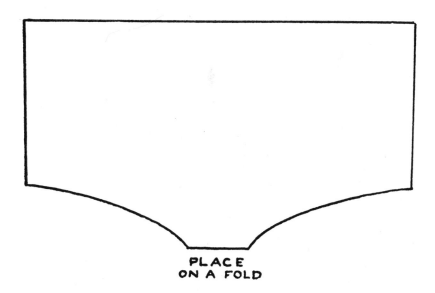

PLACE
ON A FOLD

The Baby's Clothes

Here is a pattern for panties for the baby, if you think she is old enough to wear them; otherwise, make diapers for her.

Trace a tissue paper pattern from the drawing, cut it out, and pin it on your goods to cut by.

Fine lawn or organdy is a suitable material for this underwear.

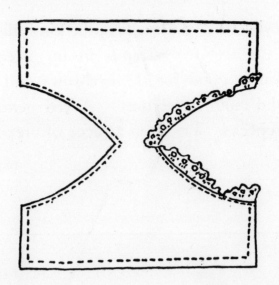

Make a narrow rolled hem around the leg openings and finish off by overhanding on it an edge of narrow lace. Hold the lace rather loosely as you sew it so it will ruffle just a little.

Make a small hem at the top of the back and front and on the sides.

Try the panties on the baby and fold two tucks, back and front, to give fullness below and also to make the waist snug.

To each corner, sew a piece of narrow tape or a "ribbon" made by cutting off the edge of the selvage of your material.

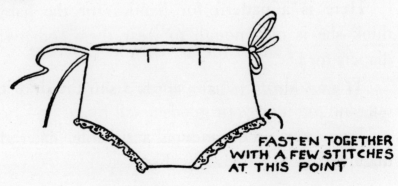

FASTEN TOGETHER WITH A FEW STITCHES AT THIS POINT

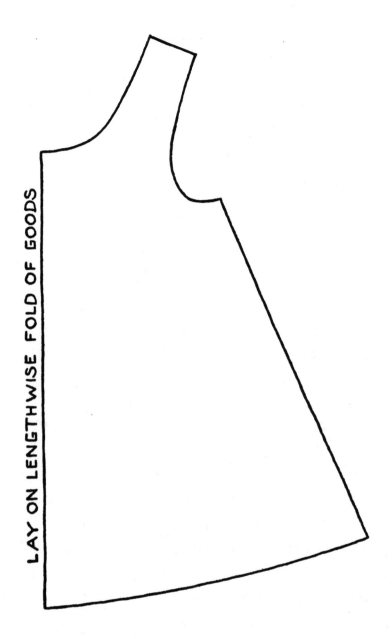

LAY ON LENGTHWISE FOLD OF GOODS

Pattern for the Baby's "Gertrude"

If you think the baby needs a shirt, use the top of this pattern.

Trace the pattern as usual and cut out two pieces. The back and front are exactly alike.

· 11 ·

Sew French seams at the side. If you aren't familiar with dressmaker terms, this means an extremely narrow seam on the right side, then turning the wrong side out, and making another seam that encloses and covers the first one. This is one of the few things I know about dressmaking.

At the neck and around the armholes make small or rolled hems.

At the shoulder make a slightly wider hem. Finish

with ribbons or a tiny button and loop. A loop seems to me easier than a button hole to make. One is shown in the drawing of the moccasin strap. A few threads form the loop and this loop is then buttonhole stitched. It doesn't matter what the stitch is as long as it holds the strands together.

Turn a narrow hem, about an eighth of an inch wide, at the bottom, and finish it off with narrow lace.

Sew lace at the neck if you wish. I don't, because the dress stays flat better over a plain finish.

A Dress for the Baby

White lawn or nainsook is the best material for the baby's dress.

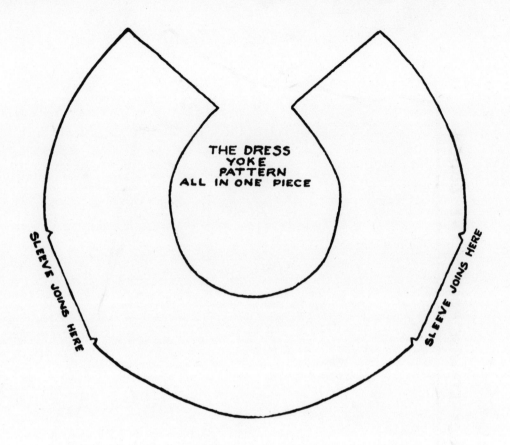

THE DRESS
YOKE
PATTERN
ALL IN ONE PIECE

SLEEVE JOINS HERE

SLEEVE JOINS HERE

Trace the drawing on tissue paper, cut it out and lay it on your material to cut by.

Indicate the notches by pencil dots instead of cutting them. These patterns are so small that notches cut in the material cause trouble in the tiny seams.

I use a single thickness of goods for the yoke, making a tiny hem around the neck, but if you prefer, and know how to seam the neck first, and turn it, you can make a double yoke.

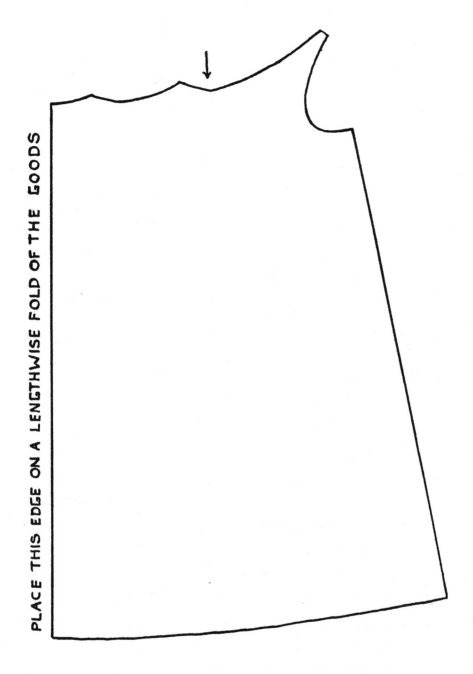

Trace this drawing on tissue paper and cut the pattern out very carefully.

Pin the tissue pattern on the folded material, and again be careful, especially around the points at the top.

The back and the front are exactly alike except that you should make a two inch slash at the center of the back so that the dress will go on easily over the feet, as a baby's dress should.

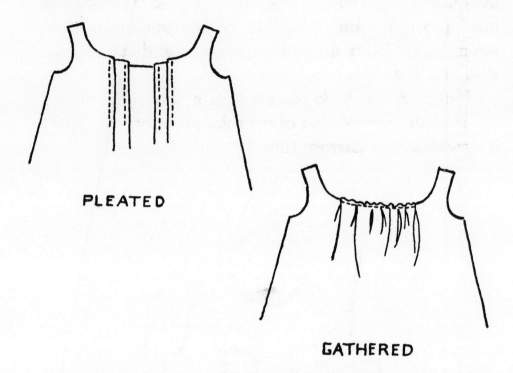

PLEATED

GATHERED

If tucks seem too hard to do, just gather the material between the arrow marks on the pattern, drawing it up to fit the yoke, as you see in the drawings above.

To make the tucks, lay the front (or back) in front of you on the table. Lift up the side with the armhole and fold toward the center making a lengthwise crease where the point sticks up high. Now baste in a tuck about an eighth of an inch wide. When you look at the right side of the dress, face the fold toward the center.

· 16 ·

I have exaggerated the point a little to help you. You can trim off any projections after the tucks are in. Do the tuck next to the center the same way, and then the one on its left side.

Next turn small hems at the back of the yoke.

To finish off the neck, cut a piece of bias facing, less than half an inch wide. Sew carefully onto the right side, making a tiny seam; then fold the bias back over to the wrong side. Turn the raw edge under and sew it down with small stitches.

Finish off the back placket with a tiny rolled hem.

Turn the outside edge of the yoke under once and baste it down—a very narrow turn.

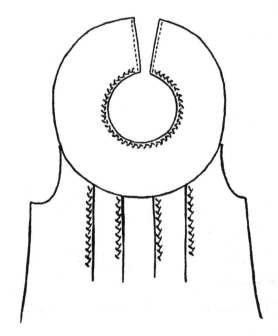

Now lay the yoke over the front so that it looks like the drawing. Baste it securely and then sew it with fine stitches on the right side. Do the back of the dress the same way.

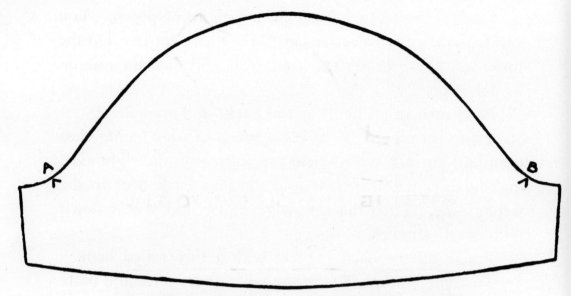

SLEEVE PATTERN FOR BABY'S DRESS

Trace the sleeve pattern on tissue paper and cut it out as usual.

Fit the curve of the sleeve to the curve of the underarm (see drawing) and sew a seam as far as the dot. Do the corresponding end the same way. Between A and B gather your material and draw it up to fit the dress, then sew the rest of the seam. Make it a strong seam so it won't rip when children tug at it.

After both sleeves are in and you give a sigh of relief (even real dressmakers hate sleeves) finish the bottoms with narrow bands.

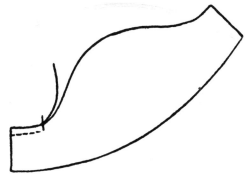

FITTING THE SLEEVE TO THE DRESS

ACTUAL SIZE OF SLEEVE BAND

SEWING THE SLEEVE TO THE BAND

Cut a strip of straight goods the size of the drawing.

When sewing the band onto the sleeve, make no gathers for half an inch at each end. The seam is on the wrong side. Next gather the center part of the sleeve and draw it up to fit the band. Do the rest of the seam.

Now turn the band back, fold under a small edge, and sew it down to cover the stitches of the seam.

· 19 ·

Next sew up the sides (small French seam) from the band on the sleeves to the bottom of the dress. You can turn the band in after, instead of before, the dress is seamed if your fingers are small.

Make a hem of about half an inch.

Finish around the lower part of the yoke, neck and sleeve bands with feather stitching. Hold the tucks that way too if you like.

Use small buttons and loops to close the back of the yoke, and the dress is done.

A Moccasin for the Baby

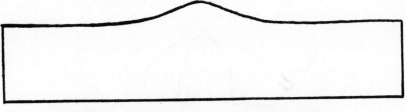

UPPER PART OF MOCCASIN

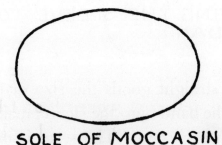

SOLE OF MOCCASIN

STRAP FOR MOCCASIN

Trace the drawings as usual on tissue paper and then cut out on the line.

Cut the moccasin out of quite heavy white muslin.

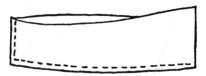

Sew the upper strip to the sole, beginning at the toe and sewing around to the heel, then starting at the toe again. Seam up the back as shown in the drawing.

Try it on the baby and gather the upper part of the toe to fit the foot.

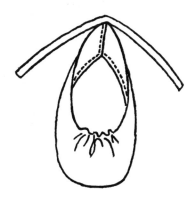

For the strap I use a narrow white ribbon folded lengthwise. Sew a small button at one end and make a loop at the other. Attach the strap at the back of the moccasin.

Instead of a strap a longer ribbon can be used and tied in a bow.

Decorate the toe with a small ribbon rosette.

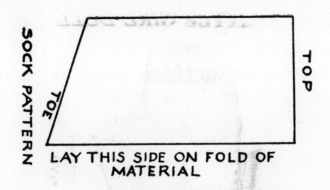

Trace the sock drawing on tissue paper. I advise you then to cut a heavier paper pattern, because it is hard to hold the pattern on the sock material. I use a real sock with a very fine weave (from the "five-and-ten") to cut mine from.

Sew small seams and make a small hem in the top, overcasting the seams.

This sock will fit beautifully if you make it snug enough.

The Pattern

CUT a piece of regular tracing paper or white tissue paper long enough to hold the full length doll—13 inches. With a pencil, trace just the upper half of the body on page 24 and then with line A coinciding with

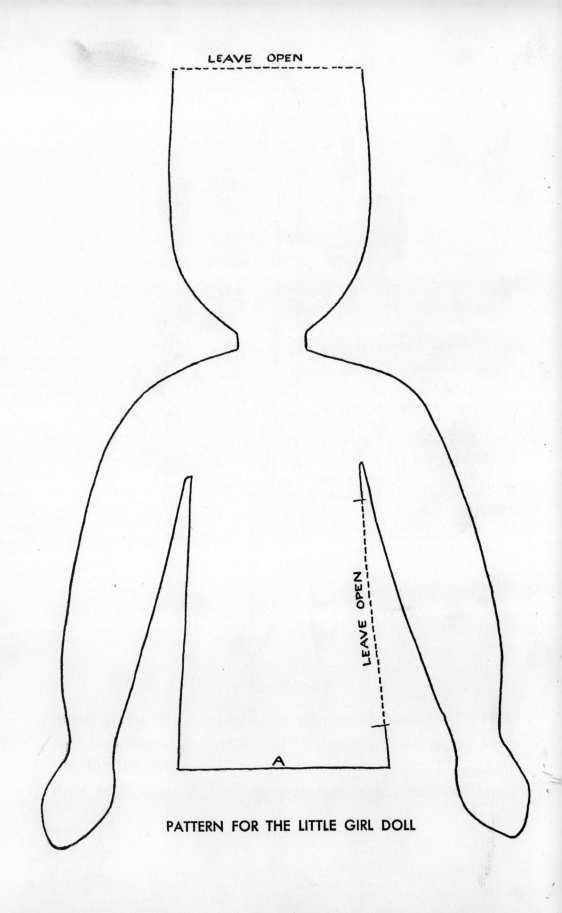

LEAVE OPEN

LEAVE OPEN

A

PATTERN FOR THE LITTLE GIRL DOLL

B

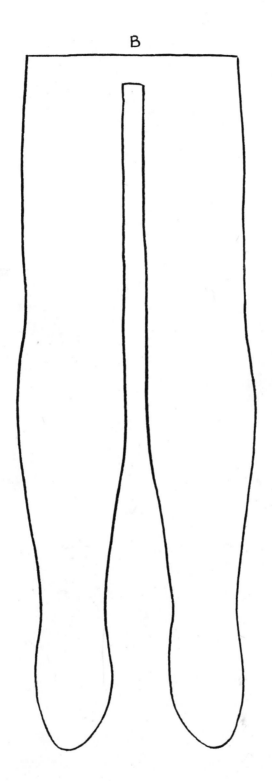

line B, trace the lower half. Cut out on the pencil line.

To make a stronger pattern that is easier to handle, place your traced pattern on a piece of drawing paper, very lightweight cardboard, or wrapping paper. Draw around it and then cut out your second pattern. It will not take long to do this and it is well worth the trouble.

It is well to be as careful as you can in making the pattern because it is so hard to be exact when you sew. You don't want one cheek to bulge more than the other.

As material for the body, I like to use a crepey material, because it will poke into shape so easily. Fine muslin will do, but use the crepe if you possibly can. It is very inexpensive. The patterns for the clothes were all made for crepe dolls. If you use muslin, try the patterns on the doll before cutting the goods because crepe stretches more than muslin.

Fold your material double so that you can cut back and front at once. Lay the pattern lengthwise on the goods, pin it or hold it firmly and then with a freshly sharpened pencil draw around it, keeping your line very light and neat.

Sewing and Stuffing

Do not cut it out yet, but sew with small stitches just inside the pencil mark. If you sew on the line instead of just inside, the black shows in the seam. Don't forget to leave a space open on one side and the top of the head.

Now cut the doll out, allowing a narrow seam about an eighth of an inch wide. Overcast each side of the neck so that it will not ravel. Cut well up under the arms and the crotch, and overcast these seams also.

Next turn the doll right side out. I turn it over the point of my scissors, starting at the toe. When I can reach it, through the side opening, I pull it through the rest of the way. I pull the arms through the side too. It saves the strain on the neck seams.

Use cotton for stuffing the body. I use inexpensive absorbent cotton. If you use small pieces at a time, you will not have any trouble. It is when you hurry that you get in a jam. Big pieces won't poke down; they leave bumps in the arms and legs.

Coax the doll into shape all the time you are stuffing it, modeling it with your fingers.

When you have stuffed the legs as far as the crotch, sew across the doll with a double thread. Leave a space without cotton at least half an inch wide, and then sew across again.

If you wish the doll to bend at the knees, leave places there too without cotton.

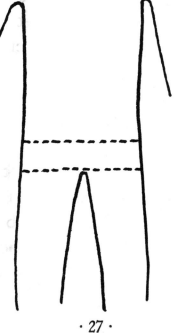

Where the arms join the shoulders, leave places the same way, if you like, to provide for free arm movement.

So many cloth dolls have floppy heads because of limp necks that I make a stiff cone for mine. A long, small headed nail, called a wire nail by carpenters, or a stick a little larger than a wooden match is perfect.

There are diagrams 1 and 2 to show you how to wrap the cotton. Wind a piece of thread around the top to hold it, then push the cone up through the neck until it fits snug. It should reach half way up, or more, into the head.

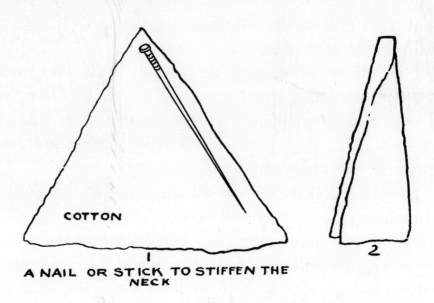

COTTON

1

2

A NAIL OR STICK TO STIFFEN THE NECK

Next finish stuffing the body and sew up the side.

Now place a smooth thick sheet of cotton between the cone and the face, and stuff in back of it—or do as I do. I keep the head rumpled down away from the cone, then wrap the piece of cotton around the cone, overlapping it in the back. I hold it well down into the neck, and I don't let go until I've pulled the face up over my fingers. Stuff the cotton in very carefully so the shape of the cheeks will be good. Fill up the rest of the head and make the top smooth and round when you sew the extra material over at the top. Keep the head quite "tall," so that the mouth won't come too low, and make the head very firm and hard.

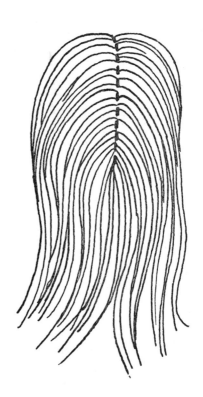

Pigtails That Can Be Unbraided

A Shetland floss with a luster makes the nicest hair for doll children, I think.

From the ball of wool, slip off a small handful of strands, then cut once across them.

Arrange the wool over the head as shown in the diagram, using ordinary sewing cotton to stitch the "part." Then braid the strands. If you like bangs, slip some strands of wool under the front and hold in place with small stitches.

You will find that you must sew the wool at the sides to keep it from slipping and showing the scalp. If your stitches are fairly tight, they will sink into the wool out of sight.

To make curls, sew the hair at the part, then take up a few strands and twist the lock until it curls back on it-self. Cut this off the right length, tuck the end up under the wool at the side of the head, and sew it so that it will lie quite flat. Do the front curls first and work around to the back.

The Face

The faces in the drawings may be traced and used to guide you. The stuffed head is a prettier shape than the paper pattern.

Remember that the curve of the cheek can be controlled by the way you put the cotton in the head.

I make the eyebrows and eyes of black darning cotton, using a simple outline stitch. The mouth and nose I make with red sewing silk or cotton. No French knots for the nose, just a single small stitch. I don't see why people are possessed to make French knots for noses! Use a red pencil for pink cheeks.

PANTIES

PETTICOAT

4½"

15"

A STRAIGHT STRIP FOR THE PETTICOAT

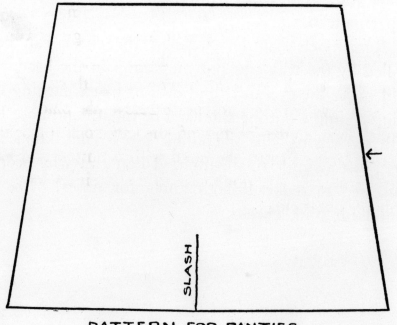

SLASH

PATTERN FOR PANTIES

Underwear

Trace the pantie pattern on the opposite page and cut out the tracing. Pin it on a double piece of thin white material, such as fine lawn, and cut out around it.

Sew one side all the way up, the other as far as the arrow.

Then sew up inside of each leg (where the slash is) and make a tiny hem in the bottom of each. Finish off with narrow lace, ruffling it a little if you like.

Turn a hem in the top, making it a shade wider than the tape or ribbon you use to draw it up with.

Cut a band for the petticoat. Have it about a half inch wide and measure the doll's waist for the length.

Where you are going to have the opening in the back of the petticoat, turn tiny hems—about one and a half inches long.

Now fold under the edges of your band. Gather the skirt to fit the band and sew it to one edge of your band in a narrow seam. Fold your band over, turn in the raw edge, and sew it down to cover your gathers.

Next sew up the back seam below the placket. Turn a small hem in the bottom of the petticoat and trim with narrow lace. Fasten the band with a button and loop, or buttonhole. If you don't like to make either loop or buttonhole, use strings.

The Dress

To make a collar like this, trace the pattern opposite, cut out the tracing, lay the pattern on a double piece of organdy. Draw around the paper with a sharp pencil.

A basting will keep the two parts from slipping.

Sew a very tiny seam (before you cut it out) just inside the line, and take the smallest stitches you ever took in your life.

For the waist, trace your patterns and cut the tracing out carefully. Lay the back on a double piece of goods

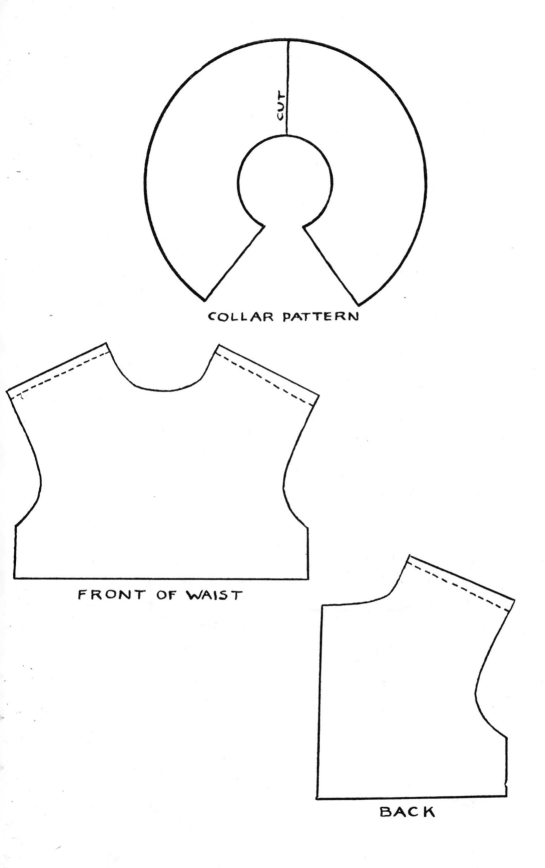

COLLAR PATTERN

FRONT OF WAIST

BACK

and pin it. Keep your mind on it when you cut it out. Cut out a single front, of course, and in the front make two small darts.

Turn hems about a quarter of an inch wide in each back.

Sew narrow shoulder seams, but do not sew the under-arm seams until the sleeves are in place.

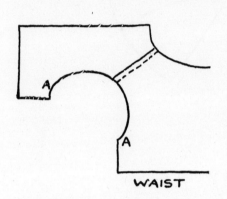

Make a tracing of the sleeve diagram and cut out your paper pattern. Pin it on a double piece of material so that you will cut both at once.

Fit the curves marked A to the same curves in the waist. Sew a small seam, then gather the top of the sleeve and pull it up to fit the top of the armhole. Sew the sleeve to the waist with a narrow seam about an eighth of an inch wide.

Now cut a band for the sleeve.

Sew each place marked B to the edge of the band, then

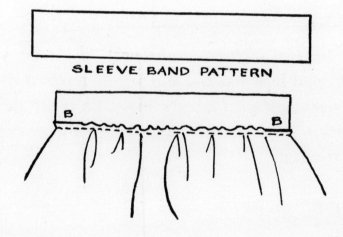

SLEEVE BAND PATTERN

gather the inbetween section to fit. Sew it to the band, fold the band back, turn under the raw edge, and sew it down to cover the gathers or you may fold it back after the side seam is done if your fingers are small.

Next sew on the collar.

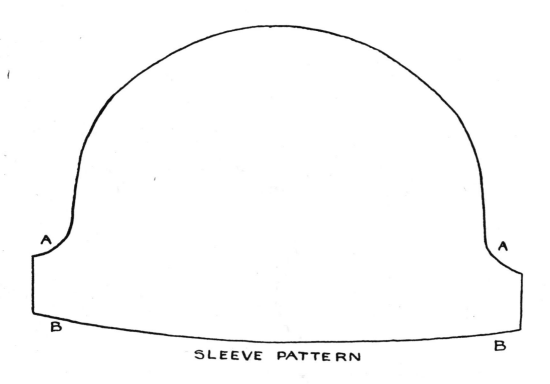

SLEEVE PATTERN

Baste the two sections to the neck of the dress, cut a narrow strip of bias material and sew on top of this. Then turn the narrow seam (and the bias with it) to the inside of the neck. Turn the raw edge under and sew it down to cover the seam.

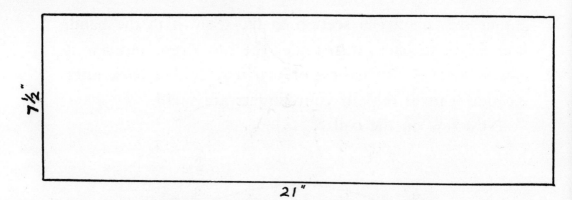

7½"

21"

STRAIGHT PIECE FOR THE SKIRT

For the skirt, cut a straight piece of goods and at each end make a tiny hem about two inches long. This will be for the placket.

Gather the skirt to fit the waist and sew it on securely, keeping the right sides of the material facing each other.

Sew up the back seam as far as the placket, then make a one inch hem in the bottom. The skirt can easily be made shorter or longer, according to the style.

Close the back of the waist with tiny buttons and buttonholes or hooks and eyes.

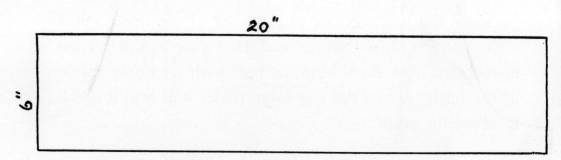

20"

6"

MEASUREMENTS FOR APRON SKIRT

An Apron

Trace the drawing of the waist on tissue paper with a pencil and cut it out on the line.

Pin the tissue pattern on your material and cut around it very carefully.

Sew the shoulder seams and hem the backs to fit the doll. Turn or roll a very narrow hem all around the top of the waist and down the sides marked "slash."

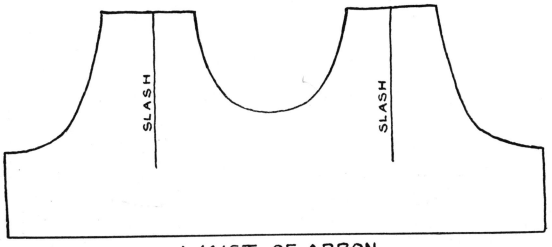

WAIST OF APRON

An "over and over" stitch of embroidery floss makes a pretty finish. You can use either a contrasting or matching color.

For the skirt pattern, cut a straight piece of material according to the diagram shown.

Make tiny hems at the back of the apron skirt, then gather it onto the waist.

Make a hem at the bottom about half an inch wide. For apron strings I tear a piece off along the selvage so I won't have to hem both sides. I'm that lazy. Have your strings nearly an inch wide and as long as you like.

A Simple Smocked or Gathered Dress

This dress is very easy to make.

Trace the drawing of the sleeve on tissue paper with a pencil. Cut it out on the line. Pin the pattern to the folded material, so you will have both the sleeves cut at once.

Keep track of the top of the sleeves. Don't get one upside down!

For the skirt, cut two pieces of material according to the diagram measurements on page 43.

In the center of the back piece, slash down from the top for a placket. Cut this about three and a half inches deep and make tiny hems.

Sew the sleeves to the main part of the dress, making a seam two inches long where it joins. You will see the mark on the sleeve pattern.

Cut a bias band for the neck about four and a half inches long and three quarters of an inch wide.

Gather the top of the dress to fit it. Try it on the doll to see where the seams should come. Sew the band on the dress with a narrow seam.

When you sew the band, remember to have the right side of the goods toward the right side of the material in the dress. Hold the gathers toward you.

Turn the band to the inside of the neck. Turn under the raw edge and sew it down to cover the stitches in the gathers.

Make bands on the straight of the goods for the sleeves. Have them at least three inches long. You had better measure your doll. Gather the sleeve, sew it to the band,

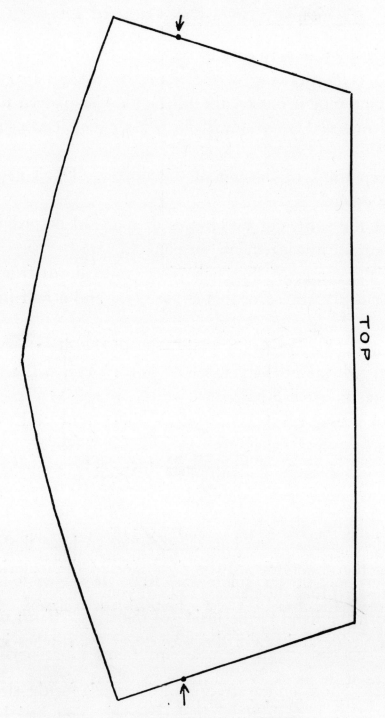

TOP

SLEEVE OF SMOCKED DRESS

· 42 ·

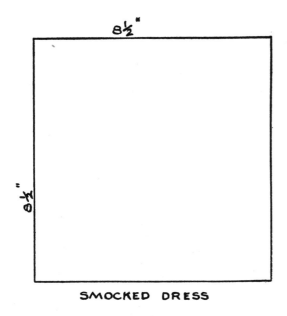

8½"

8½"

SMOCKED DRESS

HOW TO SEW SLEEVES
TO THE DRESS

then turn the band back, and fold the raw edge under. Sew it down to cover the stitches in the gathers.

Next sew up the side seams from sleeve bands to the bottom of the dress. Turn a hem to suit yourself. Close the neck with a button and loop.

If you can smock or make any fancy stitch across the gathers at the neck, it will make the dress prettier. Don't mark it for smocking, just guess.

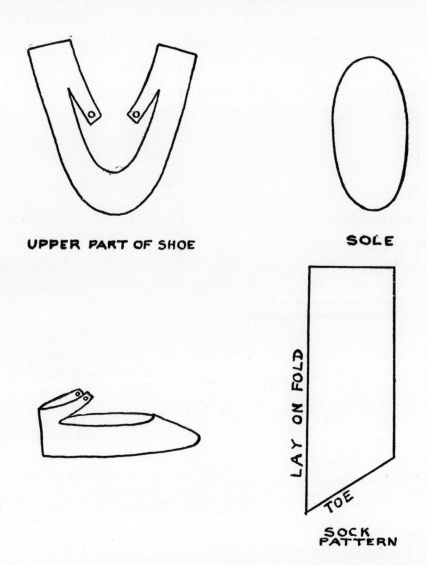

UPPER PART OF SHOE

SOLE

LAY ON FOLD

TOE

SOCK PATTERN

Shoe Pattern

Trace the patterns on tissue paper, then make heavier ones of lightweight cardboard or stiff paper.

Hold the pattern firmly on the leather and draw around it with a very sharp pencil.

I get my leather from a shoe repair man.

Sew the upper part of the sole with a fine needle and

black sewing cotton. I use number 80 or 90. Sew with an "over and over" stitch on the right side. I start at the toe and work to the heel, then start at the toe again.

Use a small black cord for the bow.

Sock Pattern

Trace the pattern as usual. Use a child's lisle sock or stocking for material, laying the long side of the pattern on a fold. This is an odd-looking pattern, but it will stretch to fit perfectly if it is snug enough. Overcast the seams so they won't ravel.

A LITTLE BOY DOLL

IF YOU would like to make a little boy to go with the little girl, use the same doll pattern as you did for her, on pages 24 and 25.

For ways to make hair for him, follow the directions given with the clown on page 67, but cut the wool very short after it is on the head. For curly hair, follow the directions given with the baby. You will find them on page 6.

The little boy's short trousers can be made of jersey or any pliable wool material, not too heavy and bulky. You can adapt the pattern which is given for the little girl's panties on page 32, or the pantalet pattern on page 55.

For a blouse, use tissue paper to get the measurements exactly right before you cut your material. To help with the shoulders and sleeves, use the patterns for the little girl's dress on pages 34 and 35. Make the waist longer, open it in front instead of in the back. Put several buttons down the front. Make the sleeves long instead of short. Make him a collar from the same pattern given for the little girl, but give him a necktie and perhaps a belt.

I have not given full directions and patterns for clothes for a boy because I have very few orders for boys. I do not know why—perhaps it is because of the materials. People love velvets and lace and gay colors. I find that I make about three hundred feminine dolls to one boy or man.

However, I think that a brother and sister doll make a nice pair for a child.

A LITTLE BOY DOLL

THE LARGE DOLL IN OLD FASHIONED DRESS

· 47 ·

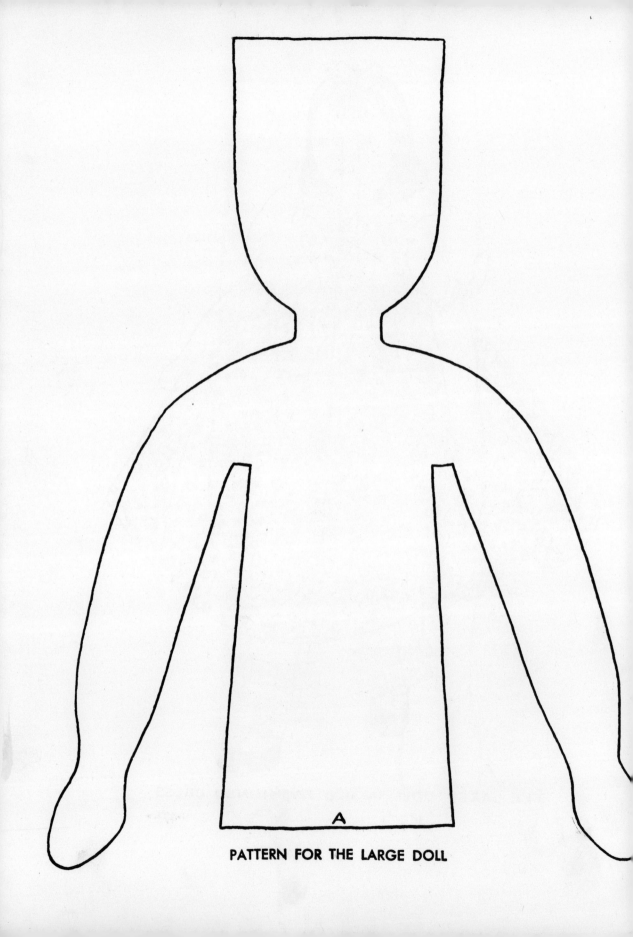

A

PATTERN FOR THE LARGE DOLL

B

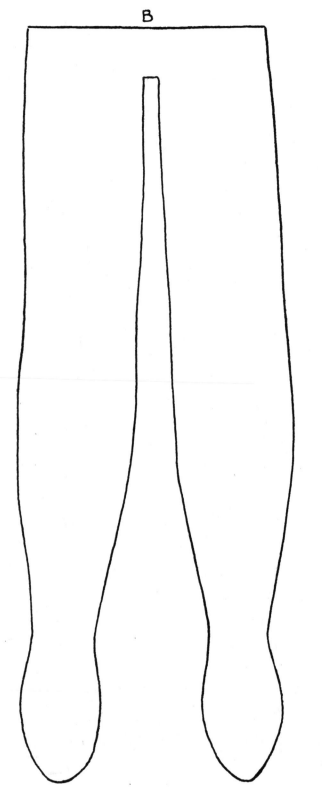

· 49 ·

THE LARGE DOLL

The Pattern

THIS pattern makes a doll about fifteen and one-half inches tall. It is a good size for a display doll or just a doll. I find that it is a size that sells well in a shop, and it may be dressed in a great variety of ways—as an old-fashioned doll, a clown, a gypsy or in any costume you choose to devise.

To make the pattern, trace the drawings on regular tracing paper or ordinary tissue paper—a sheet at least 16 inches long. Trace first the upper section and then the lower one, having the lines A and B coincide.

Cut out the tracing, place it on a piece of stiffer paper, draw around the pattern with a pencil and then cut this out on the line.

This second pattern is not absolutely necessary but it is so much easier to handle that it is well worth making.

I like to use a material for the doll bodies that "gives," so the doll can be molded into shape as the cotton is stuffed in.

Lay your pattern lengthwise on the material, which has been folded double so that you will cut back and front at once.

Be sure that the pattern doesn't slip—you can thumb tack it down if you are not working on a good table. Draw around the paper with a freshly sharpened pencil, making the mark as light as you can.

Do not cut it out yet.

Sewing and Stuffing

Sew around on the machine if you are expert (I am not) or by hand, keeping just inside the pencil line. Don't have the needle poke right through the black line.

Now cut out your material, leaving a small margin especially at the neck. Cut far up into the crotch between the legs and under the arms so that it will turn well. Overcast these places so they won't ravel. When you turn it right side out, pull the legs and arms through the side opening.

Next begin stuffing the doll. I like to use inexpensive hospital cotton best; it is smooth and clean. Begin stuffing the legs and use a small amount of cotton at a time, pressing it down firmly. Put the cotton in through the side opening.

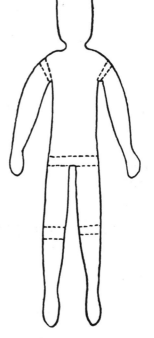

If you would like knee joints, sew across as indicated in the drawing, leaving out the cotton between the two lines of stitches. An elbow can be made the same way, but I don't like elbows except on clowns. Leave an unstuffed space at the tops of the arms too.

At the crotch leave a space at least half an inch wide unstuffed so that the doll can sit down.

After the arms are stuffed, make a hard core or cone to thrust up through the neck to keep it from bending. Have it reach halfway up into the head. To make the core I use a long nail (small head) or a stick. If I can't find a stick easily I use a kitchen match. I wrap it up tightly in cotton, winding a piece of thread around the top end. Because of the cone shape you can push it through until it fits the neck exactly.

Look at the drawing on page 28 to see how I make a cone.

Now finish stuffing the body, filling out the shoulders carefully, molding the doll into shape with your fingers. When you have filled the trunk, sew up the side opening.

Force the feet up into a human position and sew them so they will stay that way.

In the head, if you will insert a smooth sheet of cotton between the cone and the face it will help a great deal—a lumpy face is awful. Pack the cotton at the sides of the cone and back of it, being careful of the shape of the cheeks. Make a very hard firm job of the head. Pull the sides up tight when you fold over the top edges and sew them down. The doll just isn't any good if she has a soft head. Also keep in mind that a head is egg-shaped.

And still another thing: keep the head rather "tall." So many people make the head too short and then they crowd the mouth way down onto the neck, or else they lay the hair across the head just like a table runner.

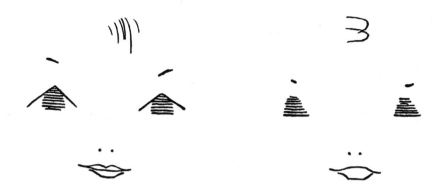

The Hair and the Face

For hair, use a fine knitting yarn. I like a Shetland Floss that has a luster. For full directions for making hair see pages 29 and 30.

There are drawings that you can trace to help you with features, but why don't you experiment with penciled ones on tissue paper? Do not mark with pencil on the doll itself—it cannot be erased.

I make eyes and eyebrows of fine black darning cotton and the mouth is red thread. The nose is indicated by two red stitches.

DRESSING AN OLD-FASHIONED DOLL

THESE patterns are made for clothes that will sew right on the body of the doll and not "come on and off." You can obtain a much better effect and if you are wondering if they sell as well, I can tell you that they do, for me. I rarely make one that can be undressed.

If you wish to make a doll for a little girl to play with, to dress and undress, make the thirteen inch "little girl" doll on page 23.

For the fifteen inch old-fashioned doll, use the patterns and directions on pages 47 to 53. When you begin to dress her, make the pantalets first. Here are measurements and diagrams to help you make a pattern.

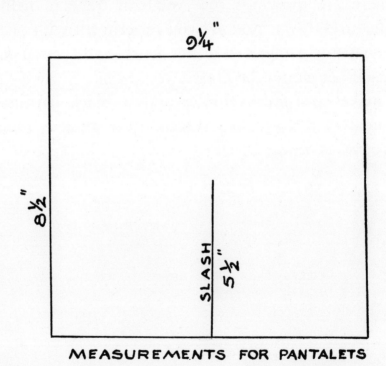

MEASUREMENTS FOR PANTALETS

Use thin white material such as organdy. Fold the outside edges to the sides of the slash and make small seams. Hem the bottoms and make two or three lace ruffles. Gather up the top to fit the doll and sew it to her.

PANTALETS   PETTICOAT

For a petticoat use the same material as for the pantalets. Cut a straight strip using the measurements in the diagram. Sew a seam up the back, make a small hem in the bottom, and finish it off with narrow lace. Gather the top to fit the doll's waist and sew it fast to her. A band on her petticoat isn't necessary.

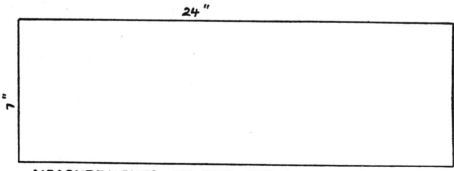

MEASUREMENTS FOR THE PETTICOAT OF LARGE DOLL

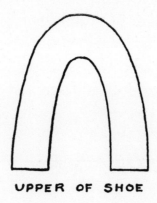
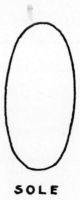

UPPER OF SHOE   SOLE

Shoes are not so hard to make as people seem to think.

Trace the drawings on tissue paper. Then from these patterns make the heavier paper ones. It will be easier for you to draw around the stiffer patterns.

Use a light-weight leather or black oilcloth. I use black leather that I buy from the nearest shoe-repair man wherever I happen to be, in the city or country. It is the kind they use to mend with.

When you sew the upper to the sole, use a fine needle and ordinary sewing cotton. A fine needle goes through the leather easily. Sew with an over and over stitch, beginning at the toe and working to the heel; then starting at the toe again. Any surplus at the back can be cut off before you make the seam.

I sew a piece of fine black cord to the back of the shoe, bring the ends around in front and tie a bow.

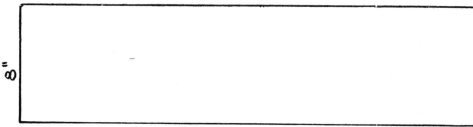

A STRAIGHT PIECE FOR THE SKIRT

Make a skirt the same way as you did the petticoat, only use the measurements given in the diagram. Turn and sew a hem or bind the bottom with a contrasting material. A strip of rickrack above the hem is pretty. Gather the top of the skirt with small stitches and sew it rather high on the doll.

On the next page is a good waist pattern. Trace the drawing on tissue paper, cut the tracing out, and use it to cut your material by.

Sew up the two darts, making very tiny seams, then fold under the lower edge of the waist, about a quarter of an inch. Hold it firmly in place over the gathers of the skirt, then turn the doll on her face on your knees while you lap the backs. Fold in one side so that there will be no raw edge. Now sew around the waist with small stitches—I think the proper term is "blind stitching." Anyway, sew the waist over the skirt and have the stitches show as little as possible. Sew the back up also, holding it away from the body. Finish the neck later.

If you are making a doll with wide puffed sleeves like the doll on page 47, cut and sew them next. Organdy is a good material. Make tiny seams. Turn the sleeve-bottoms

· 57 ·

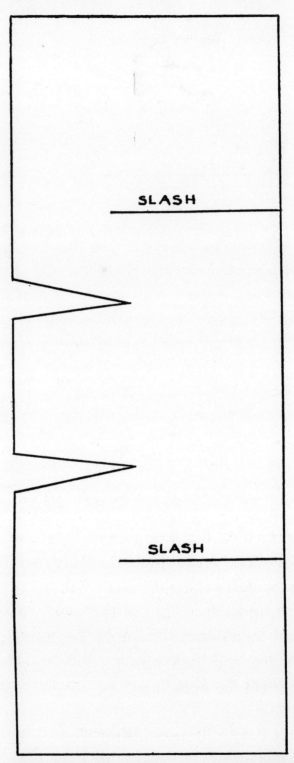

SLASH

SLASH

WAIST FOR OLD FASHIONED DOLL DRESS

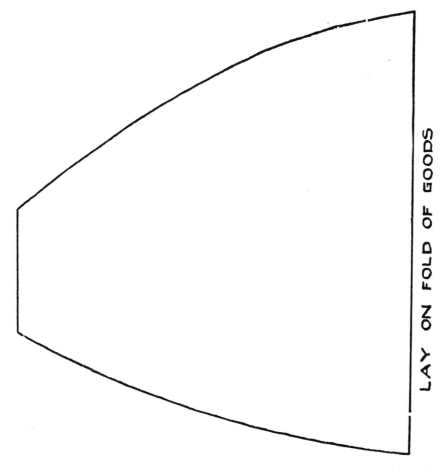

LAY ON FOLD OF GOODS

PATTERN FOR A PUFF SLEEVE

under and gather them to fit the arms, then gather the tops. Do not turn them under but sew them well up on the shoulder of the doll so that the waist will cover the gathers.

Next turn under the edges of the waist where you have "slashed" and turn under the top of the waist. If you are trimming the top with rickrack, sew this on now. Arrange the waist to cover the sleeves and sew these turned-in edges down securely.

But if you would like old-fashioned sleeves like the doll on the next page, there is a drawing from which to trace a pattern to use.

SLEEVE FOR OLD FASHIONED DOLL DRESS

In this case, finish off the neck of the dress first, curve it, and use rickrack braid, or bind it.

Next make white organdy undersleeves—straight strips of goods, each one about three by ten inches. I like to finish off the ruffle at the bottom of the sleeve with little cross stitches of color. You can use lace or just a plain little hem. Tie it at the wrist with cord, embroidery floss or ribbon. Don't bother to turn under the top when you gather it and fasten it to the arm.

Now sew up the seams of the oversleeves. Finish off the bottom with a bias binding or hem. Slip them over the arms, turn the raw edges under, then sew them to the shoulder so that the edges of the waist will be covered.

Put a row of buttons down her front, a bow on her hair, and name her.

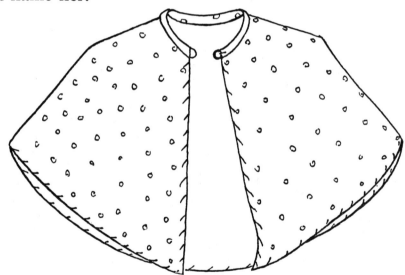

To make a cape, trace the drawing on the next page to make a tissue paper pattern.

The cape in the picture has a small hem and is overcast with black darning cotton.

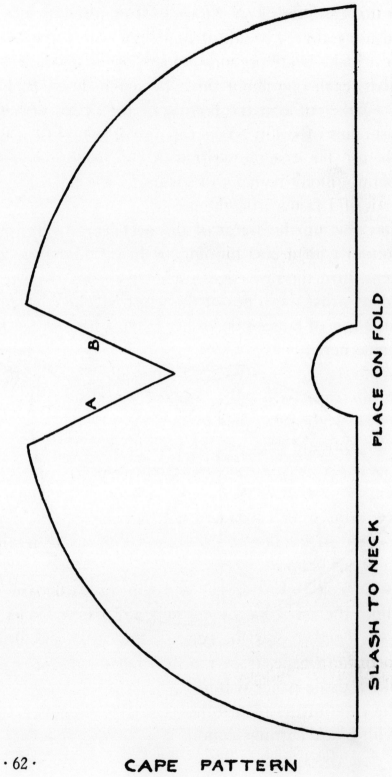

A B

PLACE ON FOLD

SLASH TO NECK

CAPE PATTERN

The neck is finished off with a narrow piece of bias of matching material. Cut it a little longer than the neck of the cape. Lay it on the cape, right side of the goods facing each other, sew a narrow seam, turn back the ends, fold the bias back over the seam, turn in the raw edge, and sew it down to cover the stitches on the wrong side of the cape.

I use a black bead for a button and make a loop of thread to go over it.

To make a bonnet pattern, trace the drawings on the next page on white tissue paper and cut them out.

Cut a piece of flexible cardboard or two pieces of heavy paper the size of the larger pattern.

Lay this cardboard on a doubled piece of material (right sides facing each other), having the straight edge on the bias of the goods so that it will curve into shape better when the bonnet is done.

Draw around the cardboard with a pencil, then sew on the line of the curve. Cut it out, leaving a very narrow seam.

Now turn it right side out and slip the cardboard inside. Fold the raw edges under and pull the two sides of the goods together over the edge of the cardboard, using tiny stitches.

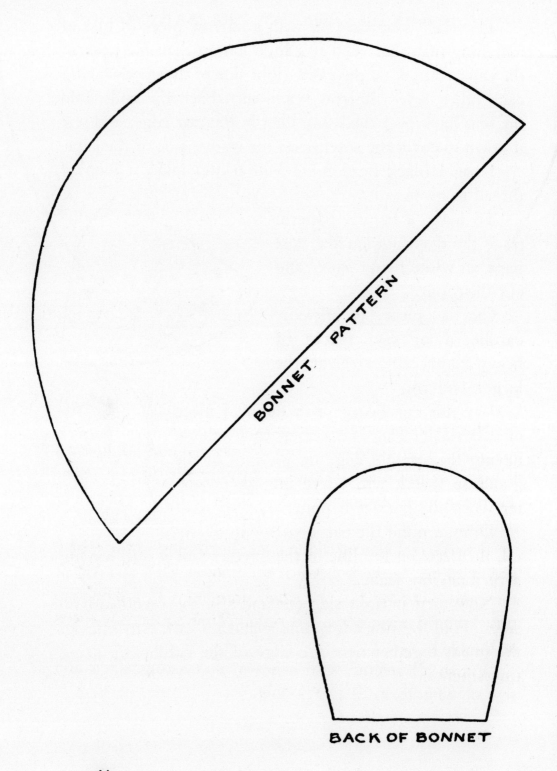

BONNET PATTERN

BACK OF BONNET

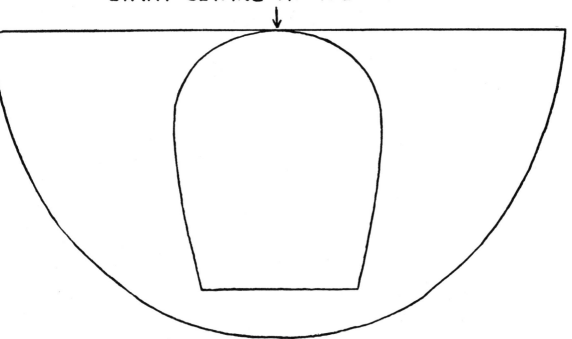

Next take the smaller pattern, for the back of the bonnet, place it on a doubled piece of material and cut around it. Sew a tiny seam around it, leaving the bottom open. Turn the piece right side out. There is no cardboard in the back of the bonnet.

Sew the front piece to the back, beginning at the center and working to the bottom of the bonnet, then starting at the center again. See the small drawing. If I didn't do this, I would never come out right. Turn in the raw edges at the back.

Finish all around with a heavy overcasting stitch and sew on ribbons to tie the bonnet.

A CLOWN

A CLOWN

USE the "large doll" pattern and directions on pages 48 to 53 for the body of the clown, but cut the arm off at the shoulder. Sew it on again after the body and arm are stuffed, using several long stitches so that the arm will swing loose like a marionette.

For the hair, cut a section from a ball of knitting yarn, Shetland Floss or some such wool, so that you have a piece about ten inches long or more, containing about twenty strands of wool.

Hold it up against the head, allowing about an inch to stick up in the air (see drawing on 68), and sew it fast with ordinary sewing cotton that matches the color of the hair. I made black hair on this one because it looked handsome with his red jacket and red and black plaid trousers. Now cut off your long end an inch from where you sewed.

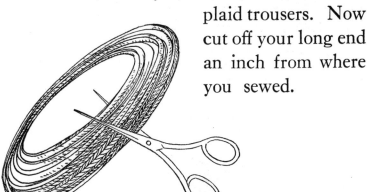

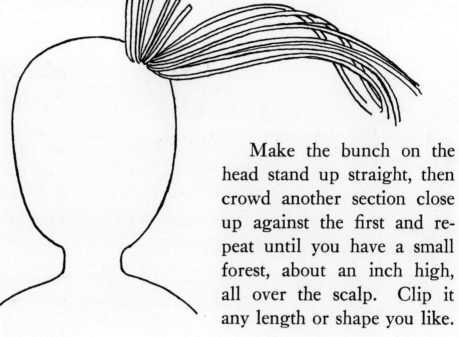

Make the bunch on the head stand up straight, then crowd another section close up against the first and repeat until you have a small forest, about an inch high, all over the scalp. Clip it any length or shape you like.

Trace the drawing to help you with features or copy a clown face from a picture in a book or circus program.

In the one I have made, the eyes are darning cotton stitches, the mouth and nose, red sewing cotton. The red cheeks and the marks on the forehead are made with a red pencil. This is a typical animal-face clown but you can make it more human-looking by leaving out the line between the nose and mouth and changing the red marks on the cheeks to round spots.

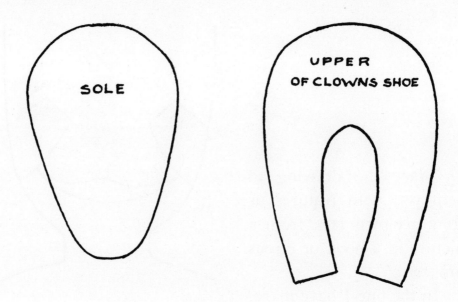

Trace the patterns of the shoe on tissue paper and from them cut some out of heavier paper. Place these second patterns on thin leather or black oilcloth, draw around them with a pencil and cut out on the line.

If you begin sewing at the toe and work to the heel, then start at the toe again, you won't have any trouble.

Use a fine needle and thread and sew with an over and over stitch on the right side.

If you use oilcloth, make an inner sole of cardboard.

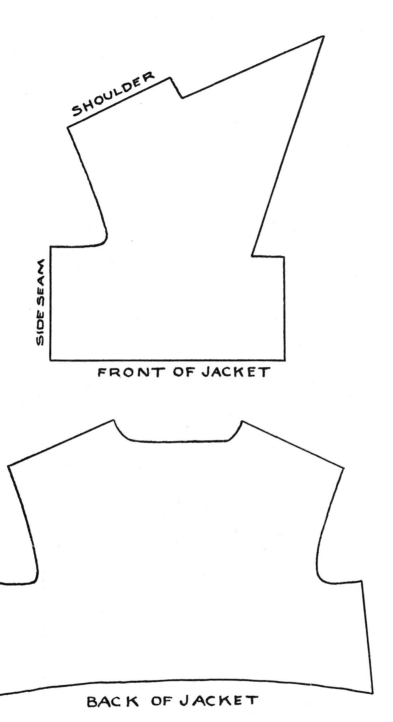

SHOULDER

SIDE SEAM

FRONT OF JACKET

BACK OF JACKET

Clothes for the Clown

Trace the drawings of the jacket on tracing paper or tissue paper, then cut them out carefully on the pencil line.

Lay the pattern for the front on a double piece of the material.

If you use a fine woven goods, like smooth flannel, you can leave the edges unfinished—hems are bulky.

For the sleeves cut straight pieces of material as shown in the diagram.

Fold the sleeve lengthwise and sew a seam for five inches. You will find that the opening at the top allows you to pull the sleeve up around the shoulder better. Gather the top and sew it fast to the doll. The jacket covers the sewing.

Make a small hem in the bottom of the sleeve and gather it about one inch from the hem to make a ruffle.

Sew the side and shoulder seams, then press back the revers or lapels.

When the rest of the clothes are on, fasten the jacket with two brass buttons. Tie a bow at the neck.

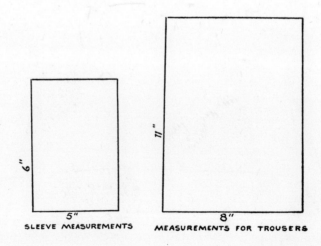

SLEEVE MEASUREMENTS   MEASUREMENTS FOR TROUSERS

For the trousers, cut out two pieces of material according to the diagram. Sew the seam of each leg for about seven inches beginning at the bottom. Try it on the clown

to see if you have it right. Trying it on will also show you how to sew the back and front seams above the crotch.

Gather the top of the trousers and cover the edges and stitches with a folded band of the same material so that it will be neat if the jacket slips up.

Hem the bottoms of the legs and gather them about an inch above the hem to form a ruffle.

There is an endless variety of clowns, Pierrots and Harlequins, and they can be dressed in silks, satins and calicoes. A handsome Pierrot is one with a black velvet cap and a suit that is half white satin and half black, or a black satin suit with a white ruff.

For that kind of suit do not use the jacket pattern but continue the upper part of the trousers above the crotch, until it reaches the neck. Have it long enough so that he can sit down.

A GYPSY

I AM VERY partial to gypsies, perhaps because they are so gay looking. I can use all the color I like and jewelry and ribbons galore!

You can make gypsies of silks and velvets or calicoes; you can have several petticoats, a voluminous skirt, with ruffles if you like. and I always have an apron, sometimes a narrow one, sometimes one that goes clear around to the back. Sometimes I make a shawl for the shoulders.

Use the large doll pattern on pages 48 to 53 for the doll's body, and refer to the directions on pages 29 and 30 for hair. Ways to do features are on page 53. I usually sew black wool hair very close to the head and cover it with a scarf or bandanna, but sometimes I make braids and wind bright ribbons in them.

Put a lot of color in the cheeks of a gypsy.

For underwear you can shorten the pantalet pattern on page 54, and use the petticoat pattern on page 55. The shoe pattern is on page 56; turn it into a pair of boots if you like by cutting a straight piece of leather, sew it like a tube, and put the shoe on to cover the bottom. Sew with an ordinary thread and needle.

The skirt should be very full. I make mine about nine and one-half inches deep and at least thirty-four inches around.

You can trim it with many bands of different colors or rickrack braid.

For a guimpe use white organdy or a thin colored material that will harmonize with, or be a good contrast to, the skirt.

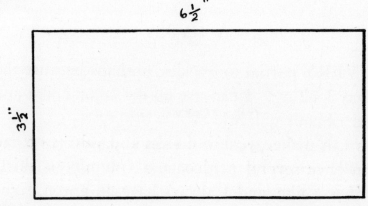

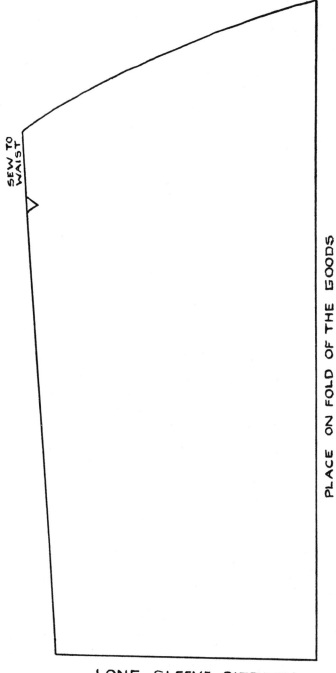

SEW TO WAIST

PLACE ON FOLD OF THE GOODS

LONG SLEEVE PATTERN

Trace the sleeve pattern on tissue paper, cut it out and cut the two sleeves by it. Just mark the notch lightly with a pencil; do not cut it.

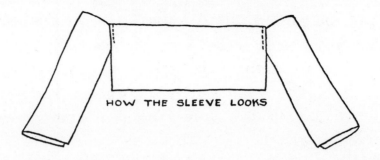

HOW THE SLEEVE LOOKS

Now cut two straight pieces of material according to the diagram, for the back and front of the guimpe.

Sew the sleeves to these pieces so that it will look like the drawing. Now sew up the sleeve seams and hem the bottoms.

Slip the guimpe on the doll and gather the neck to form a ruffle or just turn it in and gather it. I sometimes use a bright colored thread for gathering and tie a bow in front. If you do this, tie the sleeves with the same color. Gather the sleeves about three-quarters of an inch from the bottom.

Tack the bottom of the guimpe to the doll to keep it from sliding up.

A wide band of black velvet around the waist looks like a bodice. Have it over an inch wide so that it will cover the gathers of the skirt and guimpe. Put criss-cross lacers down the front if you like—use two large-eyed needles to thread the cord and cross it like shoe laces.

A good size for an apron is nine inches deep and eight inches around. Make a one inch hem and trim if it is plain material.

A gypsy gives you a chance to run riot with color but don't forget that extremely bright colors close together tend to neutralize each other. A brilliantly colored apron seems more vivid on a sober skirt.

· 78 ·

Tuck the gathers of the apron up under the black velvet band at the waist and sew it so it won't slip.

A bandanna is about the size of an ordinary handkerchief. Very often you can buy gorgeous handkerchiefs in the five and ten cent store—cotton or chiffon—that are just exactly right.

The ten cent store also has beads and jewelry—small brass rings or round brass buttons make good earrings.

DOLL-HOUSE DOLLS
The Patterns

WITH a pencil, trace these drawings on regular tracing paper or white tissue paper, then cut them out on the pencil line.

If you would like stiffer patterns, place your tissue patterns on heavy paper, draw around them, and cut out your second patterns.

If you are smart you will draw and cut these small patterns very carefully because they get out of shape a little even with the best of care, and the more precise you are with the first steps, the better the dolls will be.

The finished doll made from the father pattern, will be about eight inches tall.

If you think this is too tall for your doll-house furniture, use the mother's pattern to make the father, and then shorten mother (if you don't want her as tall as father) by cutting out a section of the pattern, about a quarter of an inch wide. The drawing will show you where to cut. Join the edges together by pasting paper on the back.

Sewing and Stuffing

Use fine white muslin for the bodies of these dolls.

Fold the material lengthwise, pin the pattern to it, or hold the pattern firmly with one hand. Draw around the pattern with a sharp pencil. Do not press too hard but keep a light line.

You aren't ready to cut it out yet. Wait until you sew it.

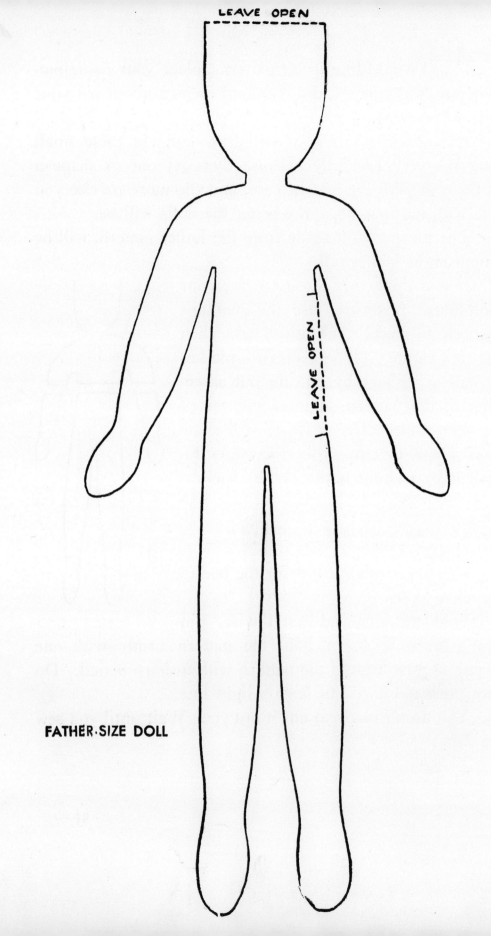

LEAVE OPEN

LEAVE OPEN

FATHER-SIZE DOLL

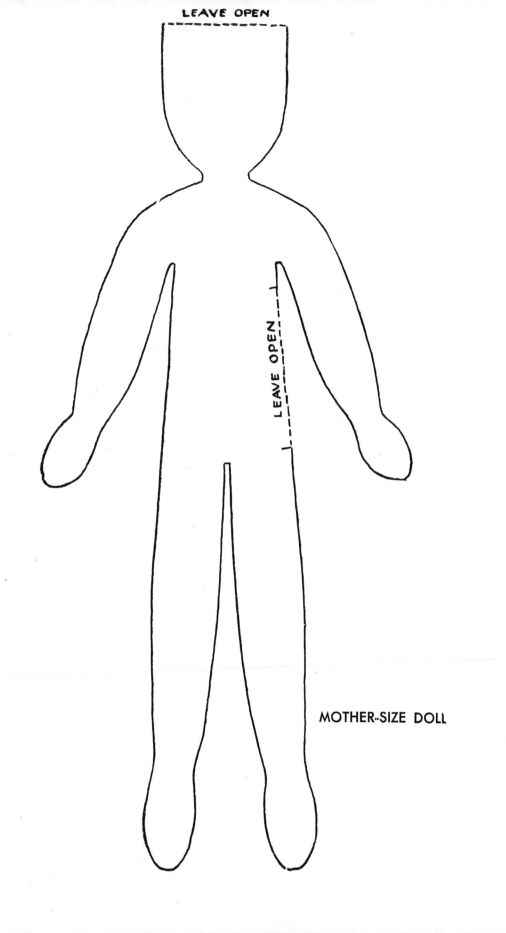

LEAVE OPEN

LEAVE OPEN

MOTHER-SIZE DOLL

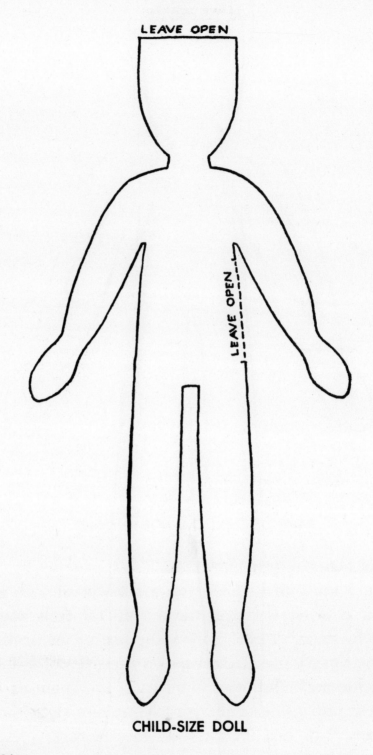

CHILD-SIZE DOLL

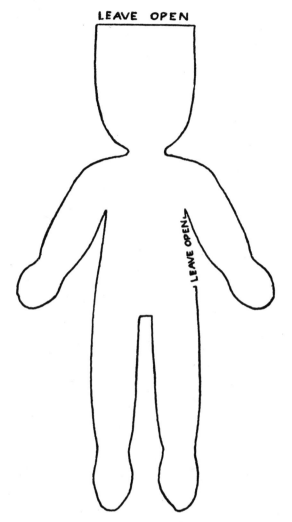

LEAVE OPEN

LEAVE OPEN

BABY OF THE DOLL HOUSE FAMILY

It is better to sew these small size patterns by hand. In fact, I think that unless you are a wizard with a machine it is better to do all the sewing for dolls and doll clothes by hand. I can't follow the line of the neck on a machine to save my life, except on life-size dolls, and the line of the neck and head is the most important of all.

I sew just inside of the pencil line, not right through it, because I do not like the seam to look dark.

After you have finished sewing, remembering to leave the top of the head and one side open, cut the doll out, leaving a small seam about an eighth of an inch wide. Cut far up into the crotch between the legs and under the arms, almost to the stitches at these points or it will not turn right side out as it should. Overcast these places and also the neck seams, so they will not pull out.

It is a miserable job to turn these small dolls right side out, but it can be done well if you don't hurry too much. You will lose your temper if you do, because you will jam up the arms and legs. You have to coax them right side out.

On the father and mother size, I use my small pointed scissors to turn the arms and legs over. I begin with a foot, pulling the goods apart with my fingers. I get it started over the closed points, then, bracing the other end of the scissors against my waist, I use both hands to coax the leg down over the scissors, until I can reach in through the side opening, get hold of the toe and pull the leg through. I pull the arms out through the sides too. If you are careful, the points of the scissors won't poke through—it wouldn't matter very much on the feet, but it would on the hands. If you would rather use a stick or a knitting needle you can, but I always use my scissors.

If you are not making a wire skeleton, you are ready to stuff the doll. Use smooth, inexpensive hospital absorbent cotton. If you put in one small fluffy piece at a time, poking each piece firmly into place (with your scissors), you won't have any trouble. Large pieces jam and make Adam's apples all over the poor thing.

When you have stuffed as far up as the knees, sew

across the leg with small stitches, leave a space unstuffed, just enough so that he will bend nicely, then sew across again. Do the same above the crotch, so that the body can sit down, and also at the top of the arms. I don't bother with elbows but you can if you would like them.

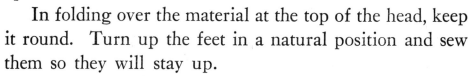

Now wrap cotton around a wooden match (light it and blow it out first), then insert it in the neck to keep it stiff. Have it reach halfway up into the head. Keep the cotton between the match and the face as smooth as possible. There is a drawing on page 28 that may help you.

Stuff the rest of the body and sew up the sides.

In folding over the material at the top of the head, keep it round. Turn up the feet in a natural position and sew them so they will stay up.

After this is done the dressing is fun. For ideas about faces, hair and dressing see the drawings given with the little girl doll or for any of the larger dolls.

To Make Wire Skeletons for Doll-House Dolls

If you want your doll-house doll to have a skeleton, the procedure is different from the point when your muslin "skin" is turned right side out.

A stranded copper wire, such as radio wire, is the finest to use, because it can be bent back and forth so many times without breaking.

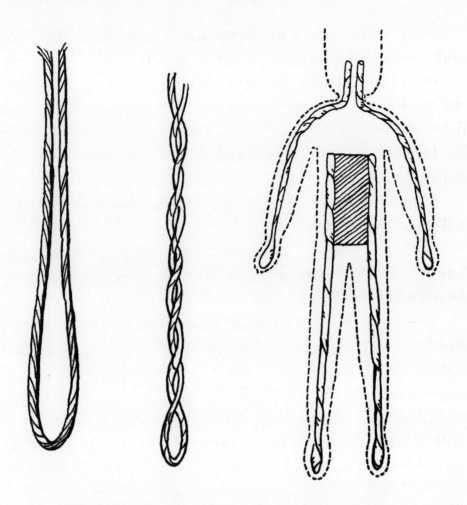

To make the leg wires, measure your doll from armpit to toe. Make a long hairpin of the wire and then twist it together. See the diagram. The loop fits into the foot.

Cut a narrow strip of muslin and wrap the wire spirally like a barber's pole.

These leg wires are fastened (with needle and thread) to a piece of cardboard which has been cut to fit the inside of the "stomach."

The cardboard keeps the legs from skidding and twisting inside of the body.

Now insert this arrangement through the side opening.

Next make two arm wires, just single wires will do, and wind these also with a strip of muslin.

Place these inside the arms, having them pass through the neck and at least halfway up into the head. See the diagram.

Be sure that the wire loops reach way down into the hands and feet.

Simply bend the feet up into natural position and they will stay that way.

After the "bones" are ready, work in just enough cotton to hold the figure in shape. Do not pack it tight or it won't bend easily.

The head, however, should be packed so that it will be firm and smooth. Fold over the top so that it is a good round shape like an egg. Sew up the side after everything else is done.

These wired dolls will take all sorts of positions and with a little support from a table or chair they can stand up.

The Baby of the Doll-House Family

I never put wire in a baby doll.

You will find it difficult to turn these very small ones right side out. If you cannot manage with something like slim scissors, try threading a long darning needle with strong thread. Slip it through the side opening. Shake it down into the toe. Pull the needle through to the outside (leaving the thread trailing out through the side opening), then remove the needle, and tie a bulky knot. Now pull on the other end of the thread, pulling the leg right side out, and proceed in the same way for the other leg and the arms.

Hair, Features and Clothes for Doll-House People

For the hair, use very fine wool that has some luster. Cut off a section of about twenty strands or wind off that much around your hand. Cut across the strands and you have a good handful of "hair" to work with.

Start with the part if you are having one. Sew the wool to the head with small stitches of matching thread. Now experiment as you might if you were a hairdresser or a barber. Work until you get an arrangement that you like. Do not be too generous with the amount or the doll will look top-heavy. Use as little as you can to get a good effect.

You will find ideas for making hair that may help you on other pages of the book. For the doll-house baby make ringlets like the ones on page 7.

Next tackle the face. If you have watercolors, they can be used very satisfactorily on muslin. Just keep your brush as dry as possible. Place a piece of tissue paper over the face and try your spacing with a pencil. Do not mark the doll if you can avoid it.

If you use needle and thread to make the features, use brown for the outline of the eyes and eyebrows. An outline stitch is best. For children, a simple dot eye is best. I've found that a blue pencil makes beautiful eyes. Just press the point in hard, and twist it around. The mouth can be made with fine red thread, and the two red stitches for the nose should be very small. Use red pencil for the cheeks.

You can always try things out on a scrap of muslin first, and it is well worth while.

When you dress these little dolls, half of your success will depend upon your choice of material.

For the man, use flexible stuff that is fine woven material that will not ravel easily on a raw edge. The fewer clumsy hems you have, the better. Make tissue paper patterns first. Start with a trouser leg. This will be just like a tube. Try it on to see how far up to sew it. You can sew a tissue paper pattern first if you are scared, but usually the material isn't valuable and you can guess well enough by holding pieces of goods against the doll. Patterns of other clothes in the book will give you the ideas.

I have made clothes for doll-house dolls so that they will come on and off, but it took a long, long time, and much patience.

Dresses should be made of material that is soft enough to cling a little to the figure. If you use stiff taffeta or satin for the mother, she won't be able to sit down. Also, the designs of the fabrics should be in scale. Chiffon and velvet are my favorite materials. As to underwear, the less the better. You might draw it on with a pencil.

Don't be afraid to try. If you choose your materials carefully you will come out all right.

Make shoes like those for the doll on page 56. Get the size by measuring the sole of your doll and making a tissue paper pattern. The shoe can be painted on, but try your paint on a sample first.

Good luck to you!

A PEASANT DOLL

CHARACTER AND COSTUME DOLLS

COSTUME dolls are a lot of fun to make. The doll itself is only nine and one half inches tall, so that small scraps of materials, silks, satins, velvets, brocades,

AN ITALIAN DOLL

etc., will make beautiful dolls. With care and thought you can make them real works of art for your own satisfaction and delight, or to sell. Doll collectors are always on the lookout for unusual dolls. It makes you feel a bit queer, though, when they ask for a doll a certain number

A FRENCH DOLL

of inches high and do not seem to care very much what it is as long as it is different from any doll they have in their collection.

Research work, looking at costumes in museums, or hunting up old pictures and illustrations is extremely fascinating. I visit all the museums I can. On a visit to Provincetown, Massachusetts, I saw a fine collection of old American costumes. There were some wonderful Eskimo clothes too, and Eskimo dolls brought to the Museum by Commander MacMillan.

In a library in Rockport, Massachusetts, I found a particularly fine book by Katherine Morris Lester. It is called *Historic Costume* and is crammed full of splendid illustrations with complete descriptions. I hope to own a copy of that book some day.

The doll can be dressed as a boy, of course, or a little old man of the woods with a green cap and a long white

beard. Put a stick in his hand and make him stoop by taking a tuck in his stomach.

The doll can be a princess with fine yellow hair falling over her shoulders, a little crown on her head, and a dress of soft apple green velvet, or an older princess in a rich blue velvet dress with lace bertha and deep cuffs. Or you may make a handsome Chinese lady, or an American bride in her dazzling satin, flowing veil and orange blossoms.

By leaving the feet down straight and making black tips of black satin or paint, you can have a ballet dancer with tarletan and flowers—and I won't be happy until I have tried my hand at making little wire hoops. Perhaps a couple in the minuet.

Then children love Kate Greenaway children, story-book children. Red Riding Hood is easy to make, and Cinderella too.

Don't be afraid to try. You ought to have no trouble at all in making the doll and by holding material on the doll and snipping and cutting, you will find the costumes easy to make.

The mediaeval lady on page 102 is only one of a dozen of that period (1400 to 1450) that I want to make. The headdresses are so picturesque! You will find the patterns and directions for this costume on pages 103 to 107.

The Pattern

Use a piece of tracing paper or ordinary white tissue paper. Trace the full-length pattern, first the upper part, then with line A on top of B trace the lower part. Cut it out on the pencil line. For a stiffer pattern take a piece of heavier paper, place your traced pattern on it, draw around this; then cut out your second pattern, which will be much easier to handle.

Keep the character of your doll in mind all the time that you are making the body. It is very easy to alter the pattern, making it a shade shorter or taller, fatter or thinner.

Place your pattern on a double piece of cotton or muslin, then draw around it with a sharp pencil. Do not cut it out yet.

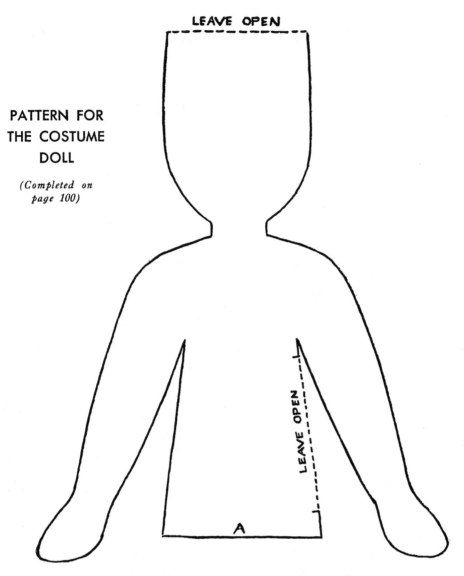

PATTERN FOR THE COSTUME DOLL

(Completed on page 100)

LEAVE OPEN

LEAVE OPEN

A

Sewing and Stuffing

Sew with small stitches just inside the pencil line. Don't forget and sew the places marked "leave open."

Cut the doll out, leaving a seam about one-eighth of an inch wide. Cut well up under the arms and the crotch of the legs. Overcast the sides of the neck, so they will not ravel. Turn it right side out.

· 99 ·

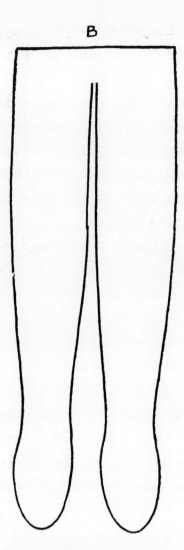

Next stuff the doll with cotton, using regular hospital absorbent cotton.

Start with the legs, and use a small piece of cotton at a time. Push it down so that it is very firm. Do the arms next. I do not put any joints in these little dolls. They look much better standing.

Now make a cone-shaped core for the neck, just a small stick wrapped in cotton to keep the neck from going limp. There is a diagram of how to make one on page 28.

Next, finish stuffing the body, filling the shoulders out well so they will be smooth and plump. Sew up the side opening.

Now you are ready for the head. Be sure and place a smooth pad of cotton next to the face and stuff the sides very carefully to keep good lines. You will see how easy it is to make one side plump and the other side lean. You can change the character of the face entirely by the way you do the sides of the head.

Pack the head so that it is firm and hard, then fold over the material left at the top and sew it down anyway you like so long as you keep the shape of a head—round, not square.

Force the feet up into a natural postion and sew them so that they will stay that way.

There is a shoe pattern for a large doll on page 56. Use that idea. Cut a paper sole the size of the bottom of the foot, then cut an upper. You can sew the paper to get it exactly right before you cut the leather. The directions with the large pattern will help you.

The Hair and Face

Hair is fun to do—always use fine wool for these little dolls and using several strands lay it on the head, experimenting until you get a becoming arrangement. The directions on pages 29 and 30 will help you.

Features are made with darning cotton for the eyes and red thread or silk for the nose and mouth. Red pencil for the red cheeks. Keep the features as delicate as you can for these dolls, and warning! tiny single stitches for the nose.

THE MEDIAEVAL DOLL.

Costume for the Mediaeval Lady

The headdress of this doll is called a great hennin, I was surprised to learn. It is made of a piece of metal brocade.

If you cut it on the bias it will stretch over the cone-shaped foundation of cardboard (or buckram) which is fastened to the head, covering every bit of hair. Mine is decorated with two strings of little gold beads.

Drape a square of fine soft net over the headdress or suspend a long piece from the point, letting it fall down over the shoulder.

The features are made with thread—not too heavy stitches. Black darning cotton, single thread, is used for the eyes and red thread for the mouth and nose. Red pencil made the rouge.

Next, cut a false under dress that will show below the tunic. It won't be as bulky and awkward as one that would go all the way up. Mine was a straight strip of soft brown velvet and I arranged it in folds, fastening the top just above the knees.

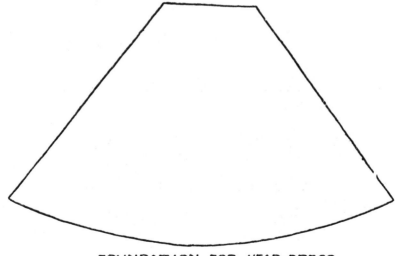

FOUNDATION FOR HEAD-DRESS

The dress or tunic is made of a piece of striped silk, brown and blue with a little red and green in the design. Planning color schemes is almost more fun than any other part of doll making.

Trace a tissue paper pattern from the drawing and have line A overlap line B.

Cut a curved or V neck, or cut it straight across. I usually cut a thing like this straight first and then shape it after it is on the doll. There is only one seam in the dress and that is down the back.

Arrange the front of the dress on the doll, turning under the raw edge of the neck or covering it with a narrow piece of velvet.

Fold the back of the dress into a couple of pleats to take care of the fullness, then turn the raw edge under and sew it securely to the doll. You may have to sew it for about an inch and a half down the back to hold it in place. Use pins first to get the effect.

To make the undersleeve, trace the drawing on the opposite page on tissue paper and cut it out for a pattern. Use brocade or velvet for the material. Turn under the raw edge next to the hand. Now wrap the material very tightly around the arm, turn one edge under and lap it over the other, sewing it in place with small stitches. This will make a snug-fitting undersleeve.

For the oversleeve, make your tissue paper pattern the same as you did for the undersleeve, but for material use silk that matches the dress.

Seam the sleeve up to within a quarter of an inch of the top. Slip it over the arm and arrange it at the shoulder,

SLASH

LAY ON FOLD OF GOODS

B

A

DRESS PATTERN

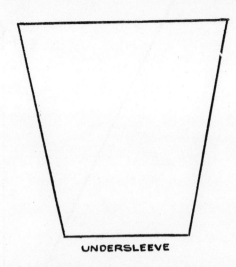

UNDERSLEEVE

turning in the raw edge at the top to cover the raw edge of the dress. Sew it fast with very small stitches.

I trimmed the dress with narrow strips of brown velvet. If you will pull a thread in the velvet to cut by and ravel out a couple of threads after it is cut, you won't need to turn in the edges of the bands.

The jewelry is a string of tiny gold beads and a piece of metal snipped from a ten cent store necklace.

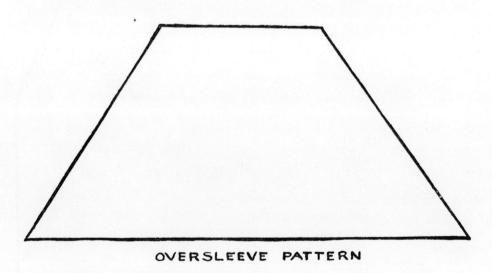

OVERSLEEVE PATTERN

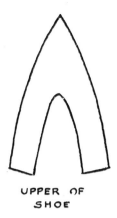

UPPER OF
SHOE

SOLE

The shoes of that period were very pointed. Cut your tissue paper patterns (trace the drawing on the next page). Then cut your kid or cloth by them. When you sew the shoes, use an over and over stitch, beginning at the toe, sewing to the heel, then starting at the toe again. Use ordinary fine sewing cotton.

After my doll was all dressed I pushed a couple of pieces of cotton way up under her dress to give her more bosom; then, as high stomachs were correct at that time, I put in more cotton to give her the right silhouette. The dress was tight enough to hold the cotton in place without any sewing.

Raise the dress if you like and fasten it to one hand.

Now that you have a lovely lady, perhaps you will place her on your mantel and in the evening in the firelight perhaps you will slip back in imagination to the early fifteenth century to the days rich in color, pageant days of velvets and jewels, chivalry and poetry.

HATS AND JACKETS

Felt Hats

ONE of the easiest hats to make is the flat, sailor type, but after you have made one you will see how other styles can be contrived with no trouble.

Cut a circular piece from an old felt hat. For the Large Doll on page 48, make it 5 inches in diameter. If the felt is black or dark color, use a red pencil.

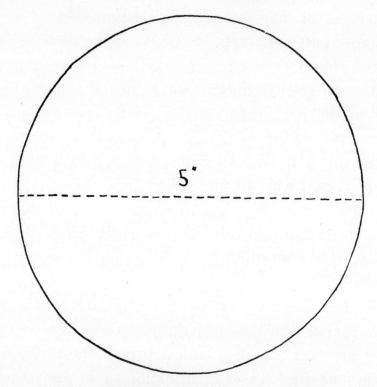

Have ready a small jar or glass to use in shaping the crown. It should be about 2 inches in diameter. A cold cream jar, a small can or glass tumbler will do.

Soak the felt in warm water about three minutes or until it is pliable.

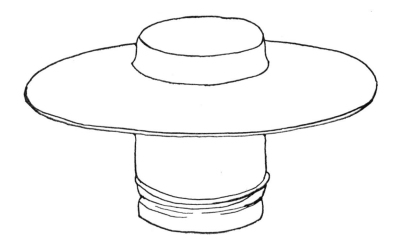

Turn the jar upside down, place the center of the circular piece on it and coax the felt down over it to poke up a crown. Keep working the brim out at right angles as you turn the hat around and around. When the crown seems deep enough hold it in place on the jar with an elastic band or a string. Now leave it alone until nearly dry.

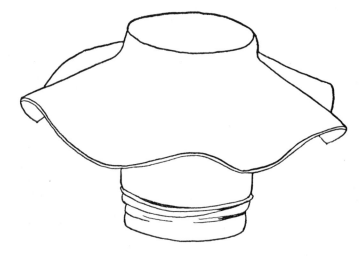

For pressing brim with a hot iron, have ready some pieces of old sheet or some such material that can be thrown away if the dye stains it.

Place a pad of the material near the edge of the ironing board, hold the hat, still on the jar, with the left hand, the thumb on top of the jar, fingers underneath. The wrong side of the felt will be up.

Place the doubled piece of material on the brim and press with a hot iron, turning and pressing until the felt will hold its shape. Don't iron it too dry or it may be marked or shiny.

Let it finish drying then take it off the jar and play with it all you like. It is better to cut it before you shape it but you can of course now cut the brim narrower—all around or just in the back.

Try it on the doll to see which shape is most becoming—try it as a tricorne, turning up three sides or try it as a bonnet turning up the back and drawing the sides tight to the head with ribbons.

Next comes the fun of fussing with flowers, ribbons, feathers and veils—see the paragraph on trimmings on page 118.

Straw Hats

Material

The easiest way to get straw braid is to rip up an old hat, your own, a friend's or one from a rummage sale. The hat can be washed (if done quickly) and sunned. The straw is usually sewn with a chain stitch which pulls out rapidly.

Choose a hat made from a very narrow braid, one quarter of an inch if possible.

Straw braid can be bought at wholesale millinery supply shops; it comes in small hanks or bundles. It is not expensive and comes in black, white, natural and some colors.

Making the Hat

The quickest way is to cut a circle out of the crown top without ripping the stitches. Moisten it in cold or tepid water and shape it as described in making a felt hat.

Size

If you wish to make a hat by sewing a crown and brim and are not certain about the size, cut a paper crown first. For the Large Doll on page 48, have the top about 2 inches in diameter. Sew a straight strip to it with over and over stitches on the right side. Try it on the doll and judge the depth. Save this pattern for future use.

Sewing

Use fine cotton thread to match the straw. Keep a shallow dish of water at hand so you can moisten a few inches of straw at a time as you work. Run your wet fingers along it.

To start the center of the crown, gather the straw braid for half an inch or so or until you can form a solid circle. If it won't draw up tight and leaves a hole, sew a piece of braid underneath or fold under the first one quarter of an inch before gathering the braid. Now overlap each row until the crown top is the right size. Taper the last inch by sliding the straw under until a smooth circle is formed then cut the braid.

To form the side, hold the straw at right angles to the top and using tiny over and over stitches sew completely around. Now go on sewing but overlap the edge of the braid as in a real hat and sew with regular stitches. You may have to poke your needle up and down, tedious work but listen to the radio if you can while you do it.

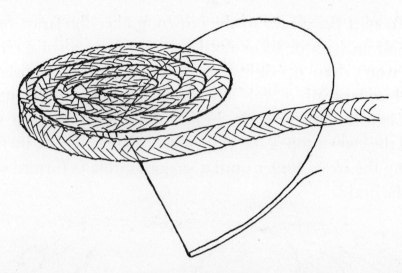

Next turn the crown upside down and start the brim with over and over stitches. Then lap the rows until the brim is the right width.

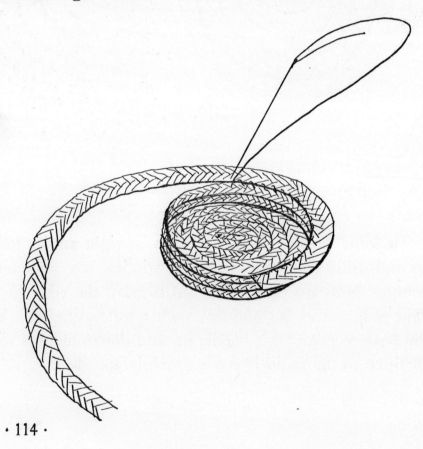

A flat pancake hat, round or oval will shape into many styles. It is especially good for very small dolls. Pinch it together in the back to form a bonnet or set it smack on top of the head. Sew a flower in the center, run a ribbon across the top (and tie under the chin) to hold the sides down. Be sure and take a stitch to hold the ribbon in place as the dolls have little or no chin.

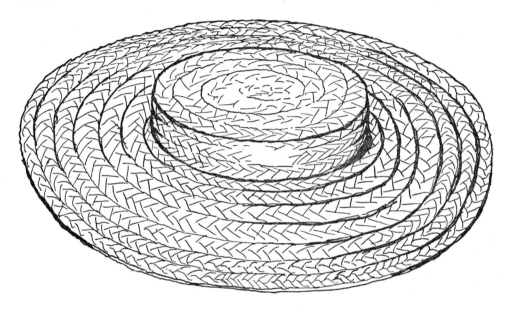

If the hat is a tiny, felt affair tipped over one eye you may find it advisable to build up the "hairdo" which is easily done by adding an extra twist of yarn.

To fashion a Poke Bonnet for a Large Doll, make a circular or oval piece for the back, add a couple of rows of braid at right angles as you did when making a crown, then build row after row as shown in the drawing or copy a real hat or picture. "Feel" the shape of the bonnet as you work, holding the braid tighter or looser to control the flair of

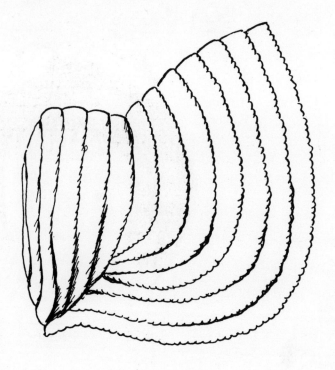

the brim. Have the last row go all the way around to make a good finish and if you would like it firmer run a second row on over it.

Straw hats can be molded somewhat when finished, by moistening the fingers and coaxing the material into better shape, or if the hat is large enough you can use an iron and press it. For the crown put a soft pad on a small jar that will fit and place a damp cloth between the crown and iron.

Ribbons of course! You can cut baby ribbon in half to use on tiny hats or fold it in half with a very sharp crease. Narrow ribbons can be cut from velvet material, too.

Instead of tying a bow on top of a very small hat, fake it, run your needle and thread through the bottom of the loops and pull it up tight.

Small flowers from the "five and ten" can be cut down with sharp scissors. Cut the petals shorter or slash each one down the center to form more petals. For years the stores have carried sprays that have tiny pink buds at the tip. I save all of these for very small hats.

I have made flowers of lovely bits of thin colored velvets. I cemented the material to white or colored note paper. When it was completely dry I drew the flowers on the paper lightly with a very sharp pencil. Try simple flowers with five petals first.

For centers I dipped the tip of a piece of fine wire in the cement, when the little blob was nearly dry I dipped it in sugar. You can experiment with other coatings. This wire was run through the center of the flower. I left the stem about an inch long. A pin point full of cement placed under the "blob" may be needed to hold it in place.

If you like, cut extra centers of white organdy, and you can touch up the petals with water color or moistened colored pencils to add variety. Try satin, silk, or paper flowers as well.

Leaves can be cut from green paper or cloth (doubled). Fasten together with rubber cement, inserting fine wire to form a stem. Experiment with a sharp pencil to see how you can deepen color and make veins in the leaves.

Jackets

Velvet jackets are very handsome on old-fashioned dolls especially on young girls as shown in Godey's Lady's Books around 1850.

A black velvet jacket with a bright red-plaid skirt of silk or lightweight wool is striking. So is a plain color velvet with figured silk skirt. But if you are using plain colors for both jacket and skirt there is an endless variety of ways to trim the costume; fringes, narrow bands of velvet on the skirt, lace collars, bows, buttons and braids on the jacket.

JACKET

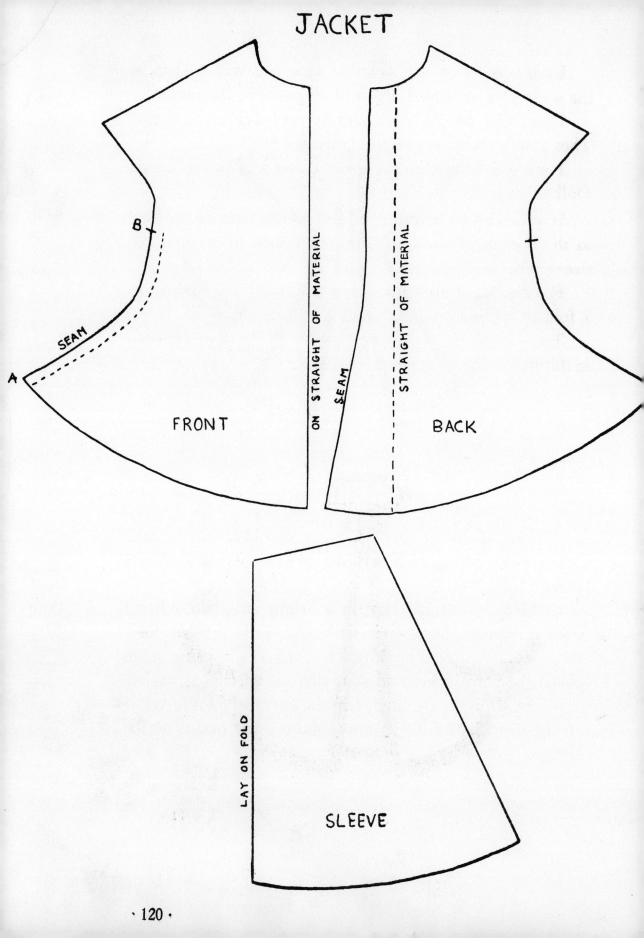

FRONT

BACK

SLEEVE

SEAM

ON STRAIGHT OF MATERIAL

SEAM

STRAIGHT OF MATERIAL

LAY ON FOLD

A

B

Undersleeves of net, lawn or lace tied with ribbon at the wrist give an added touch of elegance to the outfit.

I find that people think jackets very difficult to make. They aren't, really, as you will find out.

Here is a simple jacket pattern that will fit the Large Doll on page 48.

If you wish to lengthen it, add one quarter of an inch to the bottom of each section. Lengthen or shorten the sleeve at the bottom.

For a straight back instead of a flair, lay the pattern on a fold of the material eliminating the curve.

Trace and cut out the parts as you do the other patterns in the book.

If the material is hard to handle, baste the paper patterns to it. Leave them on until you have turned back the edges of the jacket then tear them out.

When you sew, make the back seam of the jacket first; hold it open with "cat stitching."

Sew up the side seams from A to B and "cat stitch" the same way. Make *very narrow* seams.

Now turn back (and baste) an eighth of an inch all around the outside of the jacket except the shoulders and neck. A real hem would be too bulky.

You can face the jacket with a narrow strip of bias silk or very narrow ribbon or you can hold the edge down with "briar stitching."

If you have time and patience you can line the jacket. Sometimes I line first the back, then the front sections before sewing together from A to B.

Seam and hem the sleeves (make them a little shorter than the pattern if you are using undersleeves).

Sew the sleeves on the doll and arrange the jacket in place. Turn under the front shoulders, lap them over onto the back shoulders and blind stitch. Turn under the rest and blind stitch the seams.

Now turn under the neck—use large stitches on wrong side, almost invisible ones on right.

This method gives a smoothly fitting jacket. It will be less awkward and bulky than if you sewed the sleeves into the arm holes, but if you would like to make a jacket that will "come on and off" you will not find it difficult. Try sewing your paper pattern first so you can make alterations to fit your particular doll because the way you stuff a doll can make quite a difference in the size.

PORTRAIT DOLLS

EVERY so often I am asked to make a doll that will resemble a particular girl or woman. I have always said "I'll try" because I never can see how it can be done and still look like one of my dolls which is what they wish.

· 124 ·

So far (and I have my fingers crossed as I write it) every doll has turned out most satisfactorily, and I shall tell you how I do it, although it isn't the way a professional portrait painter would go about it, I know.

All my "portrait dolls" have been made from photographs which makes it easier unless they give you six or seven and you get confused. It is better to work from two or three; a front view and one to show how the hair is arranged on the sides and back. Be sure to ask the color of the eyes and hair.

First look at the shape of the face; see if it is fat, short, long or narrow.

After the head is stuffed hold some yarn on the top to get an idea of how much forehead to cover. If at this point you think the face will be too short, which often happens, undo the top and add more cotton. Naturally you will copy the style, bang, braid, curls or whatnot.

When the hair is on I look at the eyebrows for they seem very important to me. I indicate the eyes or really put them in (carefully spaced the right distance apart), then copy the expression of the eyebrows as carefully as I can, usually with fine medium dark brown thread. Notice the height above the eyes, the thickness, the length, the tilt or the curve.

Next, notice the length of the nose and how near to the upper lip the two tiny dots for the nostrils should be.

By the way, I often split the red thread I use for the nostrils—they must not be heavy.

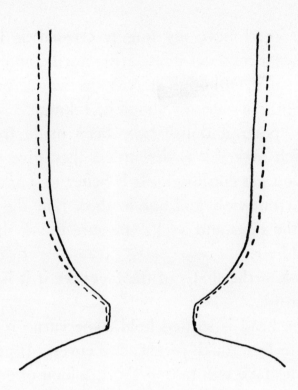

Last of all the mouth. The thickness of the lower lip is very important. The mouth being so flexible it can still look like the person whether it is turned up or down, slightly open or closed.

The main thing is to do it all with a light touch, even the color of the cheeks. If you do it all delicately, the illusiveness will allow imagination to help the resemblance.